"Once you have tasted flight, you will forever walk the earth with your eyes turned skyward, for there you have been, and there you will always long to return."

-Attributed to Leonardo da Vinci

ISBN – 13: 9798312663174

Contents

Introduction

Just over 100 years ago, aeroplanes didn't exist. We couldn't fly anywhere and the concept of getting airborne was merely a fantasy, belonging solely to those who saw the world through a different perspective. Nowadays, air travel has become second nature to most of us, with over 93,000 flights taking off every day and five billion passenger seats filled around the world each year. If you've been able to get a copy of this book, it's very likely that either yourself or someone very close to you has been on at least one commercial flight this year.

Although the act of flying is something many of us now take for granted, it's no exaggeration to say that every time people board a commercial airliner, they put their lives entirely in the hands of the pilots as they blast around the Earth at 500mph and 38,000ft in a little metal tube. The moment the aircraft door closes, passengers relinquish any sort of perceived control over their own mortality and settle in for the ride. But how much do people really know about what happens on the other side of that cockpit door?

A commercial airline pilot is one of the most glamourised but also terribly misunderstood jobs out there. Since the Twin Towers attacks in 2001, everything that happens in the flight deck goes on behind a locked, bulletproof door. It's a profession that frequently makes headlines in the media, usually when things go wrong, however, it's paradoxically become one of the most secretive roles out there. Passengers place a tremendous amount of trust into the hands of the individuals sitting on the other side of the door. Others make considerable time and financial sacrifices to be the ones seated beyond it. Still, the vast majority of people don't really know what happens within that cramped, technology-packed area in the pointy end of the jet, which we call a flight deck.

As a commercial airline captain with over a decade of experience flying passenger jets across Europe, along with a passion for writing, I think I'm in a good position to help lift the veil of secrecy and share real insights into what happens on a daily basis.

Why Did I Write This?

Whenever I'm at a social event and my line of work gets brought up (contrary to popular belief, this conversation is rarely instigated by me) I usually find myself peppered with an endless barrage of questions. It's clearly a job that seems to arouse a deep curiosity amongst many. I'm unsure whether this is due to its secretive yet glamourised nature, the lack of control most people feel on a plane, or a combination of the above. Either way, I'm often presented with an extensive list of questions about the job, which tells me there are plenty of people out there searching for answers they haven't found.

When I invested a substantial amount of time and money into my flight training, there weren't many resources out there sharing exactly what a day in the life of my future profession involved. I distinctly recall all of us trainees sitting in our flight school accommodation each evening, watching YouTube videos on repeat, which were compilations of highlights from within the flight deck. Although these videos gave us heaps of motivation to continue grinding away during the ground school phase of our training, they didn't give us real insight into the day-to-day life of the profession we were about to start.

I think it's important for anyone considering this as a career path to be given a full, warts-and-all look into what their lives could be like should they wish to embark on this adventure. This book is my way of giving something back, by sharing some of my experiences over the last decade of my life and hopefully helping others better understand what our role consists of.

Who's It For?

Whether you're a seasoned pilot with over 20,000 flight hours, or someone who's never touched an aircraft before but has an interest in flying, I've tried to write the book in such a way that it's digestible and enjoyable for all, no matter which category you fall into. It's equally applicable to those with no desire to become a pilot. Hopefully, it can bring you plenty of value and entertainment, while fulfilling your curiosity and answering your questions about what happens in the cockpit of a modern airliner.

I'll dive into the technical side of things just enough to satisfy those who are that way inclined, but hopefully not enough to lose those who aren't. For more detailed technical breakdowns of how things work, such as various approach procedures and aircraft systems, you can see my articles at PilotBible.com.

For those interested in becoming an airline pilot, unfortunately this isn't the type of role that you can shadow, or undertake work experience in. Those who want to do this job must now stump up a six-figure sum of money and devote many years of their life to flight training, before they can even step foot into the flight deck of an airliner. They must make these huge commitments without once being able to experience first-hand what a day in the life of their new potentially lifelong career actually entails. A career that I'd strongly argue is an entire lifestyle as opposed to just a job. Sounds crazy right!

To make things even harder for these potential pilots, airlines have policies restricting the taking or sharing of any photos or videos from within the flight deck, further limiting the amount of information and resources available for those that are interested. Videos that do find themselves on social media tend to be glamorised highlights of the role, with the sole purpose of getting as many views as possible. Any longer-form videos are likely to have been run past the airline's management for approval first, meaning these videos are more like promotional material, unlikely to share the true realities of the job. Unless you personally know a pilot, books and blogs are still the only way you can get an accurate insight into what we actually do each day.

When researching the very few 'a day in the life' books already published by other airline pilots, I noticed a few problems. The main one being that most of these books are very dated. Even those written relatively recently are authored by pilots at the tail end of their flying careers, who spend most of the book sharing insights into a flying era that's quite simply no longer relevant.

Aviation evolves fast, so the authors of those books are writing about a working day that looks vastly different to what my days look like now, while I'm currently operating. With the evolution of technology, along with the rise of relentless rosters and cost cutting, the average day of an airline pilot looks a lot different now than it did just a decade ago and brings with it an entirely different plethora of problems and challenges, even more so in this post-covid era.

While reading old books about the glamorous lives of airline pilots might warm the heart, unfortunately they aren't relevant for anyone interested in the modern day commercial aviation environment. I'm afraid to inform you that the 'glamorous' era for pilots is firmly buried in the so-called 'golden days'. Yet, some pilots still cling to that image, easily identifiable by their aviator sunglasses, an overpriced 'pilot's watch' (which serves no actual purpose in a modern flight deck), and often an air of arrogance about them, believing they assume a god-like status. But times have changed now, and it will never be what it was.

Enter the modern airline pilot. They tend to rock a backpack and a tired look, fully aware that their lives are far from glamorous. You'll still spot the occasional newbie who's bought into the outdated fantasy - usually rocking brand-new aviators, a flashy watch, and a car that seems impossibly beyond their pay grade. Ironically, these are often the first officers who struggle the most with both the flying and the day-to-day realities of airline life. Turns out, looking the part doesn't always mean playing it well!

Another issue with the current books out there is that the authors have their full name on them. If they're still flying for an airline, there's no doubt they've had to heavily censor or completely omit writing about certain elements of the job, through fear of job loss. A benefit of me remaining relatively anonymous is that I can include everything in this book to give you the most truthful picture possible without the fear of job loss (let's hope so anyway).

I see this as an opportunity to bring you the most up to date and accurate insights into what's going on out there. This book isn't glamorising the job. It's not trying to sell you anything. I'm just telling it exactly how it is. No sugar coating.

Why Me?

I believe it's quite a rare combination to have an airline pilot who's currently operational, with not only the time to write a book like this, but a strong desire to do so.

Over the last few years, I've attempted to hone my writing skills through blog posts for PilotBible.com, while also writing as a monthly columnist for a global aviation publication. Through this, I've developed an understanding of what audiences do and don't like to read, which has enabled me to hopefully streamline the contents of this book to the former.

This book's actually been written off the back of a popular blog post that was shared on PilotBible.com detailing what a day in the life of an airline pilot is really like. The level of engagement with that post indicated a strong level of interest in this material, so I've put it into book form, allowing me to go into 100x more detail than I could in a blog post, and share a more comprehensive insight into the role.

What To Expect

Throughout the book, I give an accurate representation of what life's like as a short-haul airline captain, operating for a low-cost carrier out of one of their largest UK bases.

In the following chapters, I've detailed two different days of the job. Both are recent real-life examples, during which I was the captain. The names of my colleagues have been changed to protect their identity, but everything else is a chronological run-through of what actually happened.

The reason for sharing not just one, but two days, is that there's so much variation in each working day. Sharing only one day wouldn't be enough to paint an accurate picture of the role.

I've specifically chosen two days that represent opposite ends of the working day spectrum. The first is a totally standard, run of the mill day. These make up 80-90% of our days. During this section I take time to detail our actions and procedures from start to finish, explaining what we do and why we do them.

Next, I share a day where things go from bad to worse pretty quickly. Days like this make up around 10% of the job, however, this one is an extreme example, jumping to the very far end of the scale. In fact, this was easily the most challenging day of my career to date, and pushed my team's and my skills to the absolute limit. I felt it important to include it as it shares insight into just how stressful the job can be, why we have to receive so much training, and essentially what we really get paid for.

During the two examples, I try to answer most of the questions I get asked on a regular basis by those both in and outside of the aviation world. Any common questions I don't answer in the examples will be shared in a section at the end of the book.

As you read, it's worth bearing in mind that life varies greatly from airline to airline and even from base to base. I know this firsthand after spending some time operating out of a very small base. Although I'm still operating for the same airline I did when I was at a smaller base, it felt like an entirely different airline altogether, due to reasons I'll dive into in the next chapter. For those interested in becoming an airline pilot, there's a high likelihood you'll operate out of a large base at some stage in your career, so I feel it's best to focus my writing around life at a big base.

It's worth noting that life while operating for a long-haul airline will also be drastically different to that of a short-haul airline pilot. At the end of this book, I go into a bit more detail about this for you.

Without further ado, let's crack on.

Day 1: The Standard Day

Rise and Shine

My working days used to start with being jolted awake in the middle of the night by the piercing sound of my alarm clock, waking me from the deepest depths of my much needed sleep. After nearly a decade of giving myself mini heart attacks each morning and combining that with the relatively newfound layer of stress added to the day job since being promoted to captain, I thought it best to do what I can to reduce the chances of heart failure and invest in a more relaxing alarm.

Today, I'm gently awoken from my peaceful slumber by the quiet vibrations of my watch alarm going off under my pillow. Unfortunately, it's still the middle of the night as far as I'm concerned. It's 3:45 am. I'm due to report at the airport in exactly one hour from now, with a 30 minute drive followed by a ten minute walk in-between me & the airport. Given that I only arrived home from work 11 hours ago and have started work pre-6 am multiple times already this week, to say I'm feeling tired would be an understatement.

As I reach under the pillow to switch the watch alarm off, I wrap myself up in the warm covers for a few more precious seconds and contemplate the idea of drifting back to sleep. Unfortunately, I know my morning routine has been optimised down to the minute (probably a skill I learnt at work) in order to maximise my sleep window each night, so there's no time for staying cosy.

I force myself straight into a cold shower in an attempt to shock my body and brain to life. Teeth cleaning happens while doing a few squats in the bathroom. Although I may look like a lunatic, it's likely the only exercise aside from walking I'll be able to squeeze in today. In my opinion, this is efficiency at its finest.

Clothes on, shoes on, and I'm out the door, grabbing my backpack on the way out. Yes…backpack. The older generation of pilots frown upon it, claiming it looks less professional than their overly large, standard issue flight bags from the 1950s with roller wheels and an extendable handle.

I can see where they're coming from, but our company allows us to have backpacks, and for me it's a much more efficient way to carry the very few things I need for my working day. All that can be found inside is my pilot licence, passport, work provided iPad, noise cancelling headset (low-cost airlines don't provide these, so we bring our own) and a high visibility vest. As you'll soon find out, we now have very limited interaction with our passengers, almost none of whom will actually see me with my bag or know that I'm a pilot, so I'm firmly part of the backpack club.

Journey In

I'm in my car 15 minutes after my alarm went off, not too shabby. When I first started flying, I'd set my alarm a leisurely hour before I had to leave the house, giving me time for a nice, relaxed shower, followed by a slow breakfast with a morning coffee. Over the years however, the increasing relentlessness of our schedules along with earlier and earlier start times, means I now prioritise getting as much sleep as I can. This means delaying my wakeup as late as possible, only leaving time for the essential tasks.

The drive this morning is quite a simple one; straight up the motorway from the south coast of England up to the London airport I'm based at. One of the few benefits of getting up at such obscene times is that we never have to worry about traffic. It's a nice feeling having the roads almost entirely to yourself. Another perk is the ability to have a sing-along during the drive in without feeling self-conscious of other drivers spectating on your solo concert. One thing that does often catch us ultra early birds out, however, is the number of roadworks that take place during the night hours. They do this to avoid any major disruption during the daytimes, so most 9-5ers won't even realise that these roadworks exist. For us shift workers though, it's not uncommon to get halfway through a journey to find the road closed for nightworks and a lengthy diversion in place. I used to allow for this and set off much earlier every morning, but with my priority now becoming maximising my sleep opportunity, I'd rather be slightly late on the very odd occasion, than have unnecessarily reduced sleep every single working day.

On today's drive, I quietly reflect on my past few days. In the last three days at work, I've suffered two engine fires, two rejected take-offs, multiple bird strikes, a brakes failure, a dual hydraulics failure, a major malfunction of all our electrical systems, along with a first officer falling ill at the controls and becoming totally incapacitated. I also had a tyre burst on the runway, and at one stage, I had an unextinguishable fire in the cargo hold and had to evacuate the aircraft. Thankfully, this was all in the simulator!

I've been undergoing what's known as a licence proficiency check. It's something all airline pilots globally have to do every six months in order to keep our licence valid. It's a multiple-day beasting, during which we have various complex failures and situations thrown at us. Quite understandably, most pilots dread it.

Displaying that you can handle very specific failures and emergency situations to a safe standard is a regulatory requirement set out by the aviation authorities. Individual airlines will often then throw further scenarios at their pilots during these simulator checks to push them up to, and sometimes beyond their limits.

The simulators these exams take place in are probably not quite what you're thinking. These are fully immersive, multi-million dollar machines that sit 15ft in the air, attached to the ground via three large hydraulically actuated legs. These legs allow the simulator to pivot and rotate as the occupants are 'flying' it, making the experience inside feel even more realistic. From the outside, these simulators could be easily mistaken for an alien spaceship.

Inside each of our simulators sits an exact replica of the flight deck from the aircraft my airline operates, the Airbus A320. Every button, knob and control is identical to that on the real thing. In place of the overcast British sky outside the cockpit windows, sits a high resolution wraparound screen, extending beyond your line of sight when you're sat in the sim. These simulators can feel so authentic that it's genuinely easy to forget you're not sitting in the real thing. It's not uncommon for pilots to leave the sessions with high heart rates and a sweaty back!

Behind the two pilot seats, sits an examiner who has the ability to control every aspect of the simulator session through an integrated computer screen, allowing them to create failures at the stage of their choosing.

As well as grading you on how you handle each scenario, the examiner has to play various roles to make the experience even more realistic. They'll often roleplay being both ATC and cabin crew, which can occasionally prove highly amusing if they're willing to put in the effort and give the appropriate accents a go!

My simulator sessions all went well this week, which I attribute to my thorough preparation. It seems mad to think that we'd have to prepare for an exam on a job that we do every day. However, much of what we face in the simulator, we only face in the simulator (thankfully!). Often, it's been six months since I last worked through some of these complicated technical failures and emergency situations, so it's a good excuse to get my head back into the books and ensure my knowledge is still as tip top as it can possibly be during the run up to the simulator exams.

At the start of my career, I used to get frustrated at the fact we essentially get tested in a high stress, high pressure environment every six months to check we're capable of doing our jobs. To be honest, I found it a little patronising. As time's gone on however, I've come to enjoy the simulator days. I go into them knowing what I want out of them, which is usually just to build my confidence up in any areas I feel need developing or that I want to become more effective in. It helps that our training department is top notch. Although I'm employed by a low-cost airline, the training they provide is certainly anything but. In fact, my airline are widely regarded as having the highest training standards amongst all airlines in the UK.

Although we can learn a lot from these sim sessions, in the back of every pilot's mind is the knowledge that if they fail a simulator check by not meeting the proficient standard, it could potentially have large ramifications on their career. Most airlines will offer you some re-training before taking another simulator exam, but understandably, if someone isn't performing on a number of consecutive attempts, the job they've devoted so much towards is likely to be terminated. It sounds ruthless, but when there's potentially lives at stake, it has to be. I'm sure it's comforting to passengers to know that we as pilots are constantly getting tested to show we're capable of handling some pretty awful scenarios.

Back to the day at hand, and thirty minutes after leaving my house, I'm swinging into the work car park. In any normal job, arriving at 4:30 am would usually guarantee you the best parking spot in the house, however, arriving at this time to the airport staff car park means you're already late to the party.

As I pass under the security gate, I notice the crew bus, which takes us from the car park to the terminal, is pulling in behind me. This means I have about three minutes to find a parking spot and walk back to the car park entrance to hop on the bus if I want to avoid the ten minute walk to the terminal. The race is on.

Our car park consists of about 30 rows, with about 50 spaces in each. Ending up at the far end of the car park is guaranteeing that I'll miss the bus. At this time in the morning, the car park is utter carnage. Cars racing round, ignoring the one way signs, all trying to find the spots nearest to the bus stop, while simultaneously trying to avoid hitting the wave of zombie-like crew staggering their way through the darkness from their cars to the bus stop.

Despite not adhering to two one-way signs and narrowly avoiding knocking over a dazed-looking cabin crew before she's even started her duty, today's not my lucky day. I end up about two-thirds of the way down the car park along with a few other disgruntled crew members who know they'll now be walking rather than getting the bus. I put my tie on in the car, grab my backpack and start the pilgrimage to the terminal, not forgetting to make a mental note of where my car is. It's not uncommon to see crew at the end of a long day wandering around the car park totally lost, while aggressively clicking their keys hoping to see some sort of orange light guiding them to where they'd parked 12 hours earlier.

The lonely walk from the staff car park to the terminal is not the most relaxing environment. It's along a main road, which is usually full of large articulated lorries and various other loud airport vehicles. It's just as well that I have no time to relax as I've already got work to be doing as I walk.

Flight Plans

When I started flying out of this base ten years ago, we'd head from the car park to a crew room. In this room, the pilots would print out paper flight plans and review them with each other. On a table adjacent to us, our cabin crew for the day would be congregating and reviewing their own paperwork, before we'd all come together for introductions and a joint brief about the day. We'd then walk out into the terminal together and head to the aircraft as a crew, fully briefed and ready to go.

In recent years, there have been a few changes to this routine, mainly in the name of time saving and cost cutting. The most notable one is that the crew room, unfortunately, no longer plays a part.

With the rise of technology, our paper flight plans became electronic, downloadable directly onto iPads that were provided to all pilots. This brought with it many advantages. One of which was the thousands of sheets of paper saved each day. Take a 60-page flight plan printed on 30 sheets of double-sided paper, multiplied by an average of 1400 sectors flown per day, that means we were printing around 42,000 sheets of A4 every day!

In light of this new tech, our company's bean counters were quick to spot an opportunity to further reduce overheads by getting rid of our crew room completely, instead turning it into an office space. Our procedures changed overnight, and we now individually head directly from the car park to our aircraft. What the accountants didn't factor in, was the impact this seemingly logical change could have on employee morale and general well-being.

While I agree it may be more time-efficient to walk through the airport solo and meet the other crew on the aircraft, it's taken a very important piece of human interaction out of the job.

Something that people may not realise is just how impersonal and lonely working at a large base can be. I've been at my base for over ten years, and can count on one hand the number of times I've flown with the same pilot more than twice. There are thousands of pilots based here, and the turnover is high, as many people move base, rank, or airline multiple times in their career, so it's very normal to fly with another pilot once and then never see them again. This means that the majority of my days are spent in a flight deck with someone I've never met before, working with four cabin crew that are also strangers.

Smaller bases with fewer aircraft can be very different to this. A few years ago, when I was at a smaller base, it was small enough for everyone to know everyone and to be consistently flying with very familiar crew. Operating out of that base felt like an entirely different job from what I do now. There was a big social scene outside of work, so being at work felt like flying with friends as opposed to strangers every day. Obviously, not everyone got along, and there were certainly some crew there who had a reputation for making days out feel much longer than they actually were. However, at least you came to know what to expect.

Due to the sheer number of staff operating at a large base, the crew room was the only place in which you'd occasionally see a face you knew, be it a pilot you'd flown with that week or one of your fellow course mates from flight training. There were also familiar faces each morning at the crew room check-in desk, along with some of the managers who had their desks stationed there. Essentially there was always at least one recognisable face to say good morning to.

Now, we often end up going days, or weeks, without interacting with anyone we actually recognise at work, so taking that little bit of regular daily human interaction away from us has made the job a lot more isolating and lonelier for sure.

There are pros and cons to both small and large bases, and each person has their own preference. While some people may thrive in the very impersonal environment of a large base, it's not my cup of tea. I prefer to know the people I'm working with each day, and for them to know me, rather than having to start from scratch every single day.

From a social point of view, I'm someone who enjoys having deep conversation and connection, so spending my days making small talk with someone I know I'm likely to never see again doesn't really suit me. Having to answer questions like "So where do you live?" every single day of your working life, starts to take its toll after almost a decade. Although the small talk questions mean well, I struggle with the concept that the person next to me quite literally knows nothing about me, and I know nothing about them, every single day. I'm often tempted to mix things up and throw out some extravagant fables about where I'm from and what I get up to outside of work, purely for my own entertainment, but I haven't yet been able to bring myself to sit and lie to the face of someone I've just met!

From a captain's point of view, another reason a large base can be challenging is that we don't really know the capacity or ability of the pilot sitting next to us. While all our pilots obviously possess a high baseline of competency and flying ability, there is huge variation in individual capacity, and how high above that baseline level of competency and ability each pilot sits. I have to try to figure this out as we go through the day. Over the years, I've worked out various indicators that can give the game away earlier in the day, but sometimes it's not possible to really know how capable the person sitting next to you is until it's put to the test.

Anyway, back to today and the work I'm starting on my walk from the car park. Contrary to what our union tells us to do, which is to not review any flight documentation on our iPads until after report time, experience has taught me there's just not enough time to sift through everything safely and thoroughly without departing late each day if we did that.

I turn the iPad on and immediately have a number of things to check before downloading the flight plan. Is the iPad OS software up to date? Is our aircraft performance software up to date? Are all our airport charts current? Legally, all of this must be up to date before we go flying.

Updates for all the above are regularly released, and it's a real pain when they're released overnight, as downloading and installing the update usually renders my iPad unusable for the rest of the walk in, losing me precious minutes. Today's a good day though, as all the software is current.

My next task, while still trying to navigate through the darkness towards the terminal without getting flattened by a lorry, is to read any 'notices to crew'. As we no longer have a crew room, it's not possible for management to tell us things in person before each duty. Instead, they're delivered directly to our iPads in digital form. These notices to crew must be checked, and any new notices read and understood before we operate each day. The system is monitored by management, who can see when you have and haven't read them. Some days there will be none, others there will be multiple, sometimes consisting of numerous pages of detail each. They can be anything from administration notices, to technical notices that could directly affect how we operate the aircraft that day. Today there's a notice about a minor upgrade to the software onboard our aircraft fleet. It takes a minute to read, but won't impact our operation today.

Now it's time to download the flight plans. Thankfully, today they download onto my iPad on the first attempt. If they didn't, it would be an indication that crewing may have swapped me to a different flight this morning. Our crewing department isn't allowed to phone us to tell us about changes to our roster when we're not technically on duty (check-in time to check-out time) as this would disturb our much needed rest. This means that sometimes the first sign they've decided to change your duty overnight can be when you're unable to download your flight plans that morning, while you're already walking into work.

My duty today is a London to Alicante and back. It's bread and butter for us. It's a route that as an airline we operate multiple times per day, and one that I've likely operated close to triple figures in my career. Today I'm just operating these two flights, otherwise known as 'sectors'. Sometimes we can operate four or even six sectors per day. A flight like Alicante could be paired with a shorter flight such as Amsterdam, which you'd complete on the same aircraft once you land back into London from the Alicante flight.

Contrary to popular belief, we don't have specific routes we always operate on, nor do we have much say over which routes we get rostered. It's all figured out using computer algorithms that are coded to utilise crew and aircraft as efficiently as possible. Every day, we tend to operate a different route, but destinations such as Alicante have such a high demand that, over a career, you're likely to operate there far more than other destinations.

Still making progress through the darkness and doing a great job of avoiding any lampposts with my attention on my iPad, I open the first flight plan. This flight plan alone is almost 60 pages long, so there's no way I can read and absorb every detail within the given timeframe. Instead, I scan the most important bits.

The first page of this document shows the technical status of our aircraft. This is where any known technical issues or defects with today's aircraft will be shown. Those not in the industry will be surprised at how many defects an aircraft can have, yet still legally be operational. It's almost unheard of for this page to be blank, and it's the same in any airline. Each aircraft type has an 'Minimum Equipment List' (MEL) created by the manufacturer. The MEL dictates which issues are a no-go and which you can still fly with, but you may require additional procedures from the flight crew or engineers for each flight. Today, our aircraft looks in relatively good nick. There are a few remarks about various minor dents on the aircraft that are likely caused by groundcrew, also a few minor snags in the cabin, but nothing out of the ordinary, so I skip to the next page.

This is the start of our actual flight plan, and here I'm scanning the following parts of information:

- The plans are dated for today, with the correct flight number.

- The aircraft registration is the same for both the outbound and inbound flights. If these were different, it would mean we're planned to swap onto another aircraft in Alicante, which brings with it other complications.

- The type and configuration of aircraft we're on today, along with any modifications it has. My airline operates three different types of aircraft: the Airbus A319, A320 and A321. These can be further differentiated into two types of engines: 'Current Engine Option'- CEO, or 'New Engine Option'- NEO. The NEOs are more fuel-efficient versions of the older engines. Each aircraft can also have sharklets or traditional winglets. 'Sharklets' look like small aircraft tails on the end of the wings. They increase fuel efficiency, but can negatively affect the handling and performance of the aircraft when landing in crosswinds. On top of this, we have a variety of cabin layouts across the fleet. I have to know all this as each aircraft and engine type has slight differences in their operating procedures.

- A quick check that our flight times are in the rough ballpark that I'm expecting. Today says 2 hours 30 minutes on the way down there which sounds about right. Occasionally, the company may re-route us around certain stretches of airspace, which can add substantial time to the flight.

- Planned take-off and landing weight. We have to bear these in mind as it could limit how much fuel we can load onto the aircraft.

- Alternate airport – The airport designated to us by the company, that we'll take enough fuel to divert into if we can't land at our planned destination.

- The planned amount of fuel for the outbound flight. I'll go into much more detail with this shortly, but for now, I'm just checking to make sure that the figure on the plan looks sensible.

- Are we tankering any fuel? Tankering is where we load as much fuel as we possibly can onto the aircraft, much more than we need for the first flight. This can sometimes be when there is no fuel available at our destination, however, it's more often because our airline has worked out on some routes where fuel is more expensive at the destination than the home base, it saves money. They have to consider the aircraft's increased weight due to the excess fuel, which will require more thrust to power it through the sky and therefore burn even more fuel. However, it's usually still cheaper to take this hit than to pay the premium prices to refuel at the destination.

Obviously, this isn't very environmentally friendly. Unfortunately, because all airlines do it, any airline choosing *not* to do it based on sustainable values would be putting themselves at a huge financial disadvantage and probably out of business pretty quickly. It's one of the many things that would require a ruling from the top in order for change to happen. In this instance, it would have to be the aviation authorities putting a ban on tankering when it's purely for financial reasons.

- Wind shear rates. This is a number between 1-12 which indicates the strength of turbulence forecast along our route. Much like most weather forecasts, it's often not that accurate. Many times, I've briefed the crew that we're expecting some moderate turbulence based on our flight plan indications, and the ride ends up being as smooth as a baby's bottom. There have also been times when the predicted shear rate has been so low that I brief how smooth we're expecting it to be, and it ends up feeling like a rollercoaster ride. I now take the shear rate number with a pinch of salt, but luckily, we have various other methods for finding out where the turbulence is, which I'll go into later.

On this first page I'm basically looking for anything out of the ordinary. If I do spot something that jumps out at me, I can investigate it further in the other pages of the plan, i.e. if there was a high shear rate, I'd look at exactly where on our routing that's expected, to figure out what's causing it and how we can best avoid it.

Next, I flick to the weather page. This shows current and forecast weather at our departure airport, destination, alternate, and a few enroute airports, taken at whatever time the plans were put together (often in the last two hours). A flick through these builds a picture in my head of how things are looking beyond the UK, as well as what the weather here is likely to do later on. The forecast for our departure, destination and alternate airports all look nice today, so I can't foresee weather being an issue. I notice a few airports on the west coast of France look pretty windy. This shouldn't affect our day, but it's nice to build this situational awareness in case we end up needing to commence a diversion mid-flight. I make a mental note to get more up-to-date weather for those airports as soon as we're in the cruise.

Then I turn to the NOTAMs (formerly Notice To Air Men, more recently changed to Notice To Air Missions after claims it was too gender specific). These are notices regarding airports and airspace. They're individually generated by each airport and contain any temporary changes or alerts that pilots need to be aware of, such as taxiway or runway closures, cranes erected near the field, or any navigation aids not working. They're also often full of very trivial bits such as planned maintenance works on areas of the airport we wouldn't be operating in. As such, there are 20 pages of NOTAMs in our flight plan today, which consist of the same array of airports as the weather forecast. It's absolutely impossible to thoroughly read these 20 pages within the timeframe we're given. On a good day, the vast majority of these aside from our departure and destination aerodrome will be completely irrelevant to us anyway. I really don't need to know that the general aviation apron in Bordeaux is having minor repair works in one corner of it between certain times today.

Frustratingly, the more important NOTAMs such as runway closures aren't automatically highlighted and are thrown in amongst the trivial ones. As such, I generally have to very quickly scan over the first few words of each line to check there's nothing in there that could ruin our day.

At this point, I look up to see two fellow company pilots walking towards me in the opposite direction. The fact they're walking towards the car park, and both look like something out of Shaun of the Dead, indicates to me they've been on a late duty and have only just landed, having flown through the night. The thought of this genuinely sends a shiver down my spine. I give them an acknowledging nod with a smile that probably screams sympathy rather than happiness. I don't get much back, but I can't blame them.

Our airline splits the days into two types of duties: early and late. When I started out, an early duty would be anything starting from 5 am through to 9 am, although most started around the 6 am or 7 am mark. A late duty would be anything starting beyond that, and tended to finish late evening, with the occasional flight finishing shortly past midnight.

Over the last decade however, earlies have started earlier, and lates have finished later. The hours we used to do would be considered a luxury now. Earlies report as early as 3:45 am, with a vast number reporting around the 4 am or 5 am mark.

Late duties now commonly finish way past midnight, some stretching right through to 6 am or 7 am, with the crew having been on duty since early evening the night before.

While making full utilisation of crew and aircraft is great for the company's profits, it's having a seriously detrimental impact on the overall health and well-being of the crew. I also believe it poses a huge safety risk, which we'll explore later in the book. I'm not sure about you, but personally I wouldn't feel comfortable or safe having to drive a car at 7 am after doing an all-nighter, let alone land an airliner!

Back to the flight plan, and I'm now looking at the pages displaying our weather charts. Although I've already reviewed the forecast for specific airports in text format, these pages now show images of the weather overlaid onto a map of our routing. It's much easier for my simple brain to comprehend at this time in the morning and helps show a more general overview of the weather en route. Again, I'm looking at any areas where we can expect turbulence and also icing, both of which will be depicted by little symbols and both of which we ideally want to avoid!

The last pages of our flight plan show any company alerts specific to both our flight routing and aircraft. This includes any noise abatement procedures for that flight, along with any notable issues that we can expect, which don't belong in our 'NOTAMs' or 'notices to crew' forms of communication.

As I come to the end of the first flight plan, all of the above is starting to build my situational awareness of what the next few hours are likely to hold, and provides me with the initial information required to make one of the most important decisions of the day; how much fuel do we want to take?

The figure I calculate in my head considers everything I've just looked at, as well as various other things such as the time of year (if it's summer, we can expect ground and airborne delays, so I'd want more fuel for this), although this is just a ballpark number which we'll refine once in the flight deck. With that number in my head and just a minute left of walking, I quickly open the return flight plan to give it an even higher level overview than the first. We have the flight down to look at this one in more detail, but I'm just checking a few bits, most notably the flight time as I know it's information I'll be asked about shortly. Quite often, you'll have a headwind going one way and tailwind the other, meaning even if you're flying the exact same route there and back, your flight times can differ significantly. Today, the winds are pretty benign at our cruising levels, so the flight time is almost exactly the same as the outbound flight.

Security

I'm now arriving at the sliding door entrance to our staff security building, so my gaze is taken away from my iPad as I tap my pass to gain access.

As I do so, I also need to get my personal iPhone out. It's the first chance this morning I've had to look at it, and I'm only doing so because I have to check-in on our company app, so that our crewing department knows I'm here on time. If I forget to check-in, I'll receive a phone call from a likely very annoyed sounding crewing officer, checking on my whereabouts. I swipe past a torrent of texts and notifications that have accumulated since I last looked at my phone yesterday late afternoon, and hit the check-in button on the app, just in time. I'm here at report time and now have exactly 60 minutes until we're due to be pushing back off the stand for departure.

Our staff security area is identical to the one passengers go through, and we're subject to exactly the same rules and restrictions as everyone else boarding an aircraft. I'd love to say I can see the logic behind this, but it's a concept I really struggle with.

Having to pick our belongings apart in order for them to be scrutinised each morning, followed by half undressing ourselves to go through a metal detector to check that we're not carrying any weapons and then be swabbed for explosive material, can be quite frustrating. Knowing it's all in the name of checking that we're not planning to bring harm to others that day, doesn't exactly make us feel like trusted individuals (a theme which you'll notice continues throughout).

It's even more frustrating when security confiscates my pot of morning oats because the level of yoghurt in there is seen as a potential threat to safety. All these security procedures fail to consider the fact that if pilots really wanted to cause harm to anyone while at work, they wouldn't require any explosive liquid smuggled through in their morning oats.

24

Not only am I about to spend the day in control of a 70 tonne jet which could easily be used as a weapon capable of mass destruction (as we've very tragically seen in the past), I'm also spending the day with access to a firefighting metal axe in the flight deck. Hmmm. I'm not sure I agree with the logic.

This morning, the security check is passed with flying colours. No water bottle was left in my bag from the previous day, and there was no selection for a more thorough search after going through the body scanner. I'm now 'airside' (before passing through security I was 'landside'). After re-packing my bag, and putting my plain black coat back on, I wander over to the information screen at the back of the security room to find out where our aircraft is parked. We have around 70 aircraft based here, and there are over 100 different spots where they can be parked. Some of the parking spots aren't connected to the terminal, which are known as remote stands. They're generally cheaper to operate from as the airport charges smaller fees to park aircraft there, but they require busses to take the crew and passengers from the terminal to the aircraft, which can often cause another headache in itself.

Today though, it's looking positive. The screen tells me the aircraft is parked on a stand that's attached to the airport via a jet bridge (although the screen has been known to deceive!) so I catch the lift up to the next floor where I'll be able to access the passenger terminal. As soon as the doors open into the passenger terminal, I'm hit with a sea of hustle and bustle. Thousands of people packed into a busy space, manoeuvring around each other at speed. People running, shouting, eating. Everyone's got somewhere to be. It's still not even 5 am so it's all quite overwhelming and stimulating for my tired senses.

I set off on my five-minute walk through the terminal and chuckle to myself about how far from the glamourised scenes of 'Catch Me If You Can' my day-to-day reality is. In the film, Leonardo DiCaprio can be seen strutting through the terminal in his pilot's uniform, surrounded by a group of extremely attractive and jolly cabin crew. As they float through the terminal they gain the awe, attention and admiration of everyone they pass. Today, I'm walking through the terminal alone, remaining as inconspicuous as possible. I'm rocking my black backpack and zipped-up coat, covering any visible sign that I'm a pilot.

25

Walking through the terminal with a captain's uniform on always draws attention, but never the type of attention you expect. I used to consistently get stopped by passengers asking questions about their flights or departure gates, usually not even for the airline I work for. It felt like I was walking around with a beacon on my head that said 'ask me anything', when in reality I was usually in a rush to get to my aircraft.

Now with my disguise on, I can make good progress through the terminal uninterrupted. It's just as well because I've got more multitasking to do.

With my focus back on the iPad today as I navigate through the terminal, I'm loading up the software that we use to calculate our aircraft's weight and balance, along with our take-off performance.

The software has various individual modules that require data input to ensure our figures are accurate. I can only get some of the data once on board the aircraft, but I can get ahead of the game here by inputting our aircraft's registration, flight number, departure and destination airports, and expected fuel figure into the iPad. Essentially, I need to get it as ready as I can before setting foot onboard the aircraft, which will allow me more time to deal with any challenges we're likely to face between now and departure.

I then start loading up our route mapping software on the iPad. I open the chart for the Standard Instrument Departure (SID) we're expecting to fly, which is listed in our flight plans. I then copy across the entire flight plan routing from the flight plan document into the mapping software, which means I'll be able to refer to our progress throughout the flight overlaid on a map.

Out of the corner of my eye, I notice the free newspaper stand and subtly slip one into my bag, this may come in handy later.

Just as the mapping software has finished loading, I'm arriving at gate 560. The gate number is revealed to the passengers around the same time I check in at security, so there are a few passengers here. I'm still undercover at the moment, so again I manage to avoid eyes and questions as I discreetly walk through the passenger seating area of the gate, before unzipping just enough of my coat to flash my ID pass to the gate staff who are preparing their computer systems for the boarding process.

Although I've never met the gate staff before, I always make an effort to smile and ask them how they're doing. I'm aware their day is mostly filled with scanning the boarding passes of passengers who probably barely even acknowledge them, along with dealing with various issues and frustrated passengers, so I think it's important to take a moment to greet them properly.

After a brief exchange with the gate staff, I'm walking down the jet bridge toward the aircraft. Although I've been doing this over a decade now, a small wave of anxiety still comes over me at this point. Nothing to do with the flying side of things, purely the fact that I'm about to meet and introduce myself to five new people that I've never met before.

Onboard

As I step on board the aircraft, there's already a hive of activity. I say hello to the cabin manager, John. He's in the middle of conducting his security search in the front galley, pulling out the canisters and trolleys to check behind them for any loose or hidden items that shouldn't be there. As expected, I've never met John before and only knew his name because I quickly checked it on our crew list on my phone while walking down the jet bridge. He seems in a chirpy mood for this time in the morning, which is nice to see, and he seems like a friendly fellow.

After the quick exchange, I notice two cabin crew down the back of the aircraft doing their security search in the rear galley. I stroll down the back to say a quick hello to Georgia and Ella. Again, both of whom I've never come across before. I know we'll have a proper brief shortly where we'll have more formal introductions, but I feel it's important to try to walk to the back and check in with them at the start of the day. Next, I head back to the pointy end of the plane and squeeze myself through the narrow entrance into the flight deck.

How Ranks Work

We have two seats in the flight deck, one on the left and one on the right. The left is occupied by the captain, and the right is occupied by the first officer. The captain carries the overall responsibility for the aircraft and everyone on board. It's their name on all the paperwork, and any decision throughout the day is ultimately to be made by them. First officers are essentially captains under training. They're there to support the captain in the safe operation of the aircraft, while also learning from them.

When you first join an airline, you'll start out as a first officer (or sometimes 'second officer' which is the same job, just a rank below). You'll take turns with the captain to fly the aircraft, but your main role will be to support and learn. At some stage in your career, you'll upgrade to become a captain, and move seats. With some airlines this move can take as little as five or six years, with other airlines it can take up to 15 or 20 years.

I spent the first seven years of my airline career walking into the flight deck and turning right, placing my rear end on the first officer's seat and working towards the day I could walk in and turn left. I certainly don't take it for granted now being able to walk in and place my bum down on the captain's seat. It sometimes still feels surreal even after doing it for the last few years. Although it took a lot of hard work and sacrifice to sit in this seat, not to mention a premature greying of my hair, I'm hugely grateful for the ability to do so.

Today's first officer, Ben, is already in his seat, and after a short exchange, he seems like a lovely chap. We engage in some non-flying related small talk but keep it relatively brief for now as we both know we're on a tight timeline and have the rest of the day to chat. We're similar ages, which is nice, and it also increases the likelihood that we'll have things in common to talk about.

As a very young first officer, the first part of my career tended to be spent sharing the flight deck with captains who were in their 40's and 50's. We often struggled finding similarities to talk about aside from flying. Now that I'm a relatively young captain, I tend to fly with first officers of the same age band as myself, which usually makes for much more enjoyable days out. It also means I quite often fly with first officers that are older than me, sometimes by multiple decades, which can make for an interesting dynamic!

Once in my seat, I reach for the aircraft technical log and flick through the first few pages of the large hardback book. Initially, I'm checking the legal paperwork required to dispatch this aircraft is all there. I then turn to the technical defects page. This should be a splitting image of what I read earlier on the first page of our flight plan file, and today it is. It's at this point that I move the tech log into the middle of Ben and myself so we can both run through it together. I've seen many captains in my time look through the entire tech log alone and in silence, without saying a word, then stow it behind their seat. This means the first officer's already totally out of the loop before the day's even begun, and actions like this can make them feel unvalued from the get-go.

Ben turns his attention to the tech log, and I confirm from it that we have no major aircraft defects to worry about today. I then flick through to the flight log pages which show where the aircraft came in from on its last flight, and what time it landed. I keep going through to the exterior inspection pages, which show the various dents and dings on the aircraft's fuselage and engines that the engineers are aware of. Unless they're fresh off the production line, every airliner will carry various small exterior defects such as dents on the fuselage (or in Boeings case, maybe even if they *are* fresh off the production line). It's also highly likely they'll have minor dents or nicks on some of the engine fan blades. It's part and parcel of operating these things. Our engineers inspect every part of each aircraft daily, noting down any external and internal defects. They'll compare what they find to the manufacturer's limits and decide whether they need to do anything about it, or whether they're safe to leave and monitor for now.

Every dent or defect found by the engineers is marked on a big picture of our aircraft in the tech log so that when we do our walkaround, we're aware of which dents and nicks have already been checked by the engineers. If we spot a new one that isn't in the tech log, it means it's probably happened between the engineer's check and us arriving on board the aircraft (likely caused by ground crew knocking ground equipment into the aircraft). In this scenario, we'd call the engineers out to come and have a look and either 'sign it off' meaning they're happy for us to go with it, or they may want to take further action.

Once we've finished reviewing the tech log, and Ben and I are both happy there's nothing in there that should prevent us going flying at this stage, it's time to decide who's going to fly which sector. As well as the two pilots being differentiated by captain and first officer, we're further labelled as Pilot Flying (PF) and Pilot Monitoring (PM).

Specific PF and PM duties will become clearer later in the chapter, but essentially PF is the one doing the physical flying of the aircraft, either via the manual controls (sidestick, thrust levers and rudder pedals) or by manipulating the autopilot. PM's role is to monitor everything PF does and make appropriate callouts if anything is beyond certain limits or they don't like what they see. PM also manages communications, be it with air traffic control over the radio, the cabin crew via the interphone, or the company via our onboard computer. PF and PM roles will be swapped between both pilots during the day, with one choosing to be PF on one sector, and therefore the other PM, then reversing roles on the way back.

An unwritten rule is that the captain offers the first officer the choice of which sector they'd like to be PF for, but there are a few caveats to this; If the weather is particularly bad at the destination, the captain will likely elect to fly that leg. Our manuals contain various limitations for the weather conditions that first officers are allowed to fly in, such as quite restrictive crosswind limits.

There are also some airports at which the company has decided only the captain is allowed to take-off or land. These tend to be airports that are trickier to operate at for various reasons such as short, narrow runways, or extreme terrain around the airfield. Examples of these on our route network are Gibraltar, Funchal and Innsbruck. In fact, for all three of these airports, captains must go through specific further training to be allowed to operate there.

Another consideration that should be made before offering up the choice to the first officer is the length of the duty, along with the time of day. If we're going to be arriving back at some obscene time after a 12+ hour day of flying and I'm with a relatively inexperienced first officer, I'll tend to operate the leg home so I'm the one doing the landing rather than a very exhausted first officer.

If I offer up the sector choice and the first officer has no preference, I've been told by a very experienced captain that it's best for me to operate the outbound sector. There's a simple reason behind this. Our company has specific Standard Operating Procedures (SOPs), which are essentially the rules we follow and the order in which we do things to operate the aircraft. Every pilot knows these and should follow them. While generally the adherence levels are very high, every captain has their own ways of doing certain things. Although these all (mostly) remain within the SOPs, it means first officers have to be very adaptable to the different captains they fly with each day, who will likely want things done slightly differently to the captain they flew with the day before. As such, the job of a first officer is often referred to as being a chameleon.

If the captain operates the first sector as PF, the first officer can see their 'style' of operating the aircraft and know roughly what's expected of them when operating the second leg, so they aren't left second guessing.

I remember the challenges of my chameleon days well, so I always ensure that I explain to all first officers I fly with that when it's their flying leg, feel free to fly the aircraft however they feel most comfortable flying it. It's their sector and I'll only interject or speak up if I think safety is at risk. If I see anything that I believe could be done in a much better or more efficient way, and would be constructive to share, I'll usually do this at the end of the day rather than while they're flying.

There have been many times in my career where I've had captains 'fly through' me, a trait that can be tremendously frustrating. This is when you're trying to fly the aircraft, how you feel comfortable, but the captain is telling you what they want you to do with the aircraft's trajectory, before you've even had a chance to do it yourself. They'll also interject with various other ways that you're not doing things how they like it done. You can end up feeling like a puppet.

More often than not, the next day you'll be operating with a different captain. You'll do things how you were instructed to do by the captain ie previous day, only to be met with criticism from the current ̶pɩain, who'll tell you to do things their way.

It's a game you can't really win. While SOPs are great for keeping things generally standard and mitigating the worst of the above, you'll still end up feeling like a chameleon sometimes, it's just part of being a first officer.

Today, Ben explains he'd like to take the aircraft out to Alicante as he's been flying the London-bound legs of his other flights this week. It can get quite monotonous always being the one to do the landing back at home base, so I resonate and tell him it's all his!

Preparation

It's time to refine my answer to the big question that could decide the fate of our day, 'How much fuel do you want?'.

First officers know that when captains ask them this question, it's a slightly rhetorical one. I have the fuel figure I calculated in my head from earlier, and that's the absolute minimum amount of fuel we'll be taking regardless of what Ben says. If, however, Ben's figure is higher than mine, and he has a valid reason for it, I'll gladly go with his higher figure.

Fuel is our lifeline in an airliner. It buys us time and keeps us alive. Unfortunately, it's also rather expensive! If we choose to fill the tanks today, there will be a £50,000+ invoice heading the company's way.

Quite understandably, all airline pilots are encouraged in one way or another to only take the fuel they think they really need. Any excess fuel that isn't used costs the company extra money and emissions by flying an unnecessarily heavy aircraft on that leg.

While some very low-cost airlines have been known to seriously pressurise and even penalise their pilots who take excess fuel, thankfully my company has a very sensible towards it. While we are strongly encouraged to seriously think about the validity of taking any fuel beyond that which the flight plan says we'll need, never in my ten years with this company have I been questioned by management on a decision to take extra fuel.

Obviously, as pilots we want to do our bit too. We want to save the company money while also trying to keep emissions down, so we calculate a fuel figure that seems sensible enough to keep us out of trouble, but without putting an unnecessary amount of fuel on.

The fuel figure calculated by our airline and presented on our flight plans includes predicted fuel for the following:

- Taxi fuel – to get us between the parking stands and the runway.

- Trip fuel – fuel from take-off to landing at intended destination, flying the planned route and altitudes.

- Alternate fuel – to get us from a go-around at our intended destination, to landing at our alternate landing airport.

- Contingency fuel – 5% of the trip fuel, which allows for variation in wind predictions and minor changes in our routing, essentially acting as a buffer to ensure the 'trip fuel' will be adequate.

- Final reserve fuel – 30 minutes worth of fuel. This fuel should never be touched and acts as a final barrier to fuel deprivation. If you ever have to use any of this fuel, you're having an extremely bad day, but you're also going to have to explain your actions to the authorities.

On top of this, we have the ability as pilots to add 'extra fuel'. Although on a standard day, the above will be sufficient fuel to get us safely to our destination, my experience in aviation has taught me that no day is standard. There are always problems that arise, some of which can't be anticipated. These problems tend to always take time to sort, which inevitably equates to fuel.

Problems that can be anticipated tend to be mostly weather related. If you're flying somewhere with poor weather, you can expect delays getting into the airport as aircraft will be diverting around the weather or conducting multiple approaches. If it's foggy, ATC may have to put larger gaps between aircraft on the approach, adding further delays. If there's bad weather or turbulence expected en route, you may end up climbing and descending to try and avoid the worst of the turbulence, or you may end up deviating laterally off your planned route to avoid thunderstorms. During summertime in London, you can almost guarantee you'll be given a slot that delays your take-off time, so you'll end up burning more fuel on the ground. You're also more likely to enter the airborne hold on your way into any busy airport. All of the above will require more fuel so if you're anticipating it, you should add extra fuel appropriately.

Back when I was a first officer, I once had my captain elect to take the fuel designated on the flight plan from London to Amsterdam, despite Amsterdam weather data showing heavy thunderstorms. I told the captain I wanted more fuel as thunderstorms would usually mean arrival delays, whereby we're told to hold in the air, therefore burning lots of fuel. For a reason still unbeknown to me, the captain refused my proposal.

Sure enough, just over an hour later as we approached Amsterdam airspace, we were told to enter the airborne hold for 25 minutes as a minimum. With no extra fuel, we burnt our contingency fuel while we remained in the hold for five minutes, in the hope that they may cancel our holding. Then we were down to just our alternate and final reserve fuel remaining. We had to request a diversion to Rotterdam due to lack of fuel, which frankly, felt embarrassing after being in the hold for just five minutes. It was a show of poor airmanship from the captain, and probably not enough pressure from me as a first officer to take more fuel. At the end of the day, I knew when the captain refused to take extra fuel that safety wouldn't be at risk, as the alternates were clear of weather so I wanted to see how it played out. It was also a great example of a time where pilots need to take initiative and put more fuel on than the flight plan says.

In terms of the accuracy of our planned fuel, our airline cleverly uses data from the previous flights on the selected route, to calculate how much fuel those flights actually ended up using 99% of the time. They'll take these statistics and alter the flight plan fuel to reflect this. Although it's handy to have this data, the company states that they'd rather we divert 1% of the time due to not having sufficient fuel to hold for unexpected delays, than be carrying around excess unused fuel on 100% of our flights.

Diversions can be expensive and lengthy for passengers and crew, but someone at the airline has worked out that operating 1,400 flights per day, all carrying unnecessarily high fuel loads, is more expensive than a few of those flights diverting to refuel. In the example above, however, there was no excuse to not take a substantial amount of extra fuel when we could anticipate a major delay.

Today, Ben verbalises the logic leading up to his fuel decision. "The weather in Alicante is nice, no turbulence or weather expected enroute, but we're likely to get a slot out of here so maybe a few hundred extra kilograms of fuel for that, to give us an extra 20 minutes on the ground?".

He presents a figure that matches what I had in my head. Perfect. Ben flips the very old school numerical flip chart stowed in his side of the flight deck to '7.5', and wedges it in his cockpit side window, indicating to the fueller who's already arrived outside the aircraft that we'd like 7.5 tonnes of their finest Jet A1 fuel.

It's now time to power up the aircraft's electrical systems. So far, everything's been nice and quiet in the flight deck, but that's about to change. I reach up to the overhead panel and switch on the aircraft's batteries while also pushing the ground power button. This allows the aircraft to be supplied by a ground-based generator, saving our batteries from being depleted before we've started our engines. Once started, the engines will become our source of electrical generation.

The flight deck suddenly springs to life. Screens start flickering and flashing, all running self-tests. Various dings and chimes emanate from the loudspeakers as systems are starting up. At the same time, our ears are treated to a whirring sound, similar to that of someone turning a hairdryer onto a low setting. We know this noise is now here to stay for the duration of our day. Various blowers and vents have all kicked into operation to circulate the air around the avionics bay, which is right beneath us. While it's great to know the important avionics are being kept from overheating, it creates a surprising amount of background noise in the flight deck.

A few years ago, there was a stage where we were ending up with lots of aircraft in the hangar, unable to fly due to damaged avionics. It took a few months to figure out what was happening. A trend had started where pilots were turning off the noisy avionics blower fan whilst on turnarounds, to bring a bit of peace and quiet into the flight deck. Unfortunately, and unbeknown to them at the time, they were frying the extremely expensive avionics below them!

Over the background noise produced by our avionics fans today, I hear John introducing himself to someone in the front galley, so I turn in my seat to see our fourth cabin crew member, Joel, boarding the aircraft. I say a quick hello through the thin space separating the cockpit from the cabin, then turn back to continue the set-up of the aircraft.

Ben jumps out of his seat to conduct the flight deck security search (a duty designated to the first officer in our airline). He's checking in all the nooks and crannies of the flight deck for loose articles, or things that simply shouldn't be there. Any doors and hatches must be opened, and items removed to check behind them. He's essentially mirroring what the cabin crew are doing. It's a legal requirement by the authorities (in this case the UK's Civil Aviation Authority - CAA) to conduct this thorough check at the start of the day. The CAA have been known to occasionally plant dummy explosive devices in various concealed places in the flight deck or cabin, to test the meticulousness of our searches. Fail one of these tests and you've got some serious explaining to do.

I meanwhile shine my torch underneath my rudder pedals to check there's nothing behind them to stop them reaching their full deflection if needed during the flight. You'd be surprised at what you can find behind there! I then test my oxygen mask by pressing buttons in a certain order to check whether oxygen is being supplied to the mask, and then test whether the built-in microphone is working. If we have a depressurisation or a fume or smoke event onboard the aircraft, these masks will be our saving grace.

By now, the small computer screen next to my right leg on the central pedestal has flickered fully to life. The official name for this is little gem of technology is a 'Multi-functional Control Display Unit' or MDCU for short, but I shall refer to it from here on out as 'the box' as that's how airline pilots refer to it. The box consists of a small screen, along with an alphabetical and numerical keypad below it. There's one on my side, and one on Ben's side. Both look identical, and they're the interface we use to access our Flight Management Guidance Computers (FMGCs). I'll try to go easy on the acronyms, but everything in aviation has an acronym, so please be understanding! I promised not to get too technical so to keep it light, the FMGCs are central to the aircraft's incredible ability to navigate itself through the skies.

I prod a few buttons on the box to request a current weather report from our departure airport. A few seconds later, a small printer, also on the central pedestal, springs to life. It starts spewing out printed text on a small slip of paper. I peel the slip off and place the fresh report between me & Ben, who's now finished his security checks.

Our procedures require us to input the data from this weather report into our performance modules on our iPads, to find out what our maximum take-off weight will be on the current runway in use, with the current weather conditions, before we continue with too much more set up. We then crosscheck this figure with each other, while confirming we both have the correct aircraft registration selected in the module. If there were any issues here in terms of being too heavy, we may end up having to re-think our fuel decision. If we simply needed to take as much fuel as we were putting on, yet the software was telling us we'd be overweight, we'd have to request a different routing from flight planning, or even worse, kick passengers off this flight. Today is all good, as we'd expect. We have a huge runway here in London, and we've never been limited by its length. The procedure for checking the bigger picture weight-wise is more for smaller airports with unfavourable weather conditions that will negatively affect take-off performance, but our SOPs state we must do it before every flight. Later in the setup, we'll refine these performance calculations once we get the passenger and baggage information.

Speaking of, another new face now boards the aircraft and comes into the flight deck. It's our dispatcher, Paul. Paul's role has different names at different airlines, but with us he's called a Turnaround Coordinator (TCO), or a Dispatcher. His role is to be the liaison between various parties while the aircraft is parked on stand: The pilots, cabin crew, gate staff, baggage handlers and several other ground staff servicing the aircraft. As a passenger you'll definitely have seen a dispatcher, they're always wearing high vis jackets and usually rushing in and out of the flight deck looking very stressed. They are usually under a lot of pressure from their management to get the aircraft away for an on-time departure.

As you may have come to expect by now, I've never seen Paul before. We exchange hellos and he hands us a 'load sheet'. This sheet of paper shows the actual number of passengers checked in, along with how many of them are males, females and children. We use a standard weight for each category and are also shown the distribution of where the passengers will be sat (our cabin is divided into three zones for our paperwork). The load sheet also shows how many bags will be loaded into each of our three cargo holds, and how much they weigh. We'll need all of this data to accurately calculate our take-off speeds and the aircraft's centre of gravity.

That part of the set up will have to wait, because at this point, the cabin manager, John, walks into the flight deck and says he's ready for our brief. This means the cabin crew have finished their security checks and are ready for us to come and have what's known as an 'interactive brief'.

Crew Brief

The point of this brief is to pass essential information about the day onto the cabin crew, but it's also a chance for us in the flight deck to connect with them, and for me as the captain to assess their level of fitness to operate that day.

As I leave the flight deck, all four cabin crew are now sitting in the passenger aisle seats in rows 1 and 2. The more traditional captains will stand up at the front of the aircraft in the middle of the aisle and give a monologue of what they think the crew want to know. Think teacher – student style. They'll often do this while completely unaware that they're totally obscuring the first officer who's awkwardly stuck standing behind them, or behind a cabin bulkhead, unable to see the crew and feeling very left out of the loop.

I like to do things a little differently. I jump into row 1 and sit myself on an armrest by the window, facing the crew. The reasons for this are multiple fold. By doing so, I've brought myself physically down to their level, which hopefully shows that before I've even said a word, I very much believe we are all a team and all equal, as opposed to an 'us and them' attitude that some pilots have. It also leaves room for the first officer to be fully visible at the front, which feels more engaging and inclusive. I believe it also portrays a friendly, relaxed vibe from myself as opposed to adopting an authoritarian stance in front of them. At the end of the day, we're all aware of who has the overarching authority here, but I'm a big believer in the idea that a good captain is one that doesn't need to make this hierarchy noticeable, unless you have a situation in which authority is suddenly required.

As the captain, it's my job to run the brief and I try to keep it as interactive as possible. I ask all the crew how they're doing, trying to acknowledge each of them individually rather than collectively. I check to see if anyone was called off standby, as this may affect the maximum hours they can work today. I then introduce our first officer along with myself, and proceed to share the highlights they're all waiting for: flight times, expected weather conditions or turbulence, any defects that could affect them, and anything else out of the ordinary.

Today's pretty plain sailing, so there are no collective sighs at an unexpectedly long flight time one way, or turbulence that could disrupt their service. There are no defects in the cabin for me to discuss with the crew today, so cabin manager John goes straight into reciting to me where each crew member will be working onboard the aircraft, along with what sort of security procedure they're expecting to do in Alicante. At some airports, the crew must do a full security search in the cabin before we depart, as they did this morning. At others, it's not necessary.

Then John asks arguably the second most important question of the day: "What would you like to eat and drink?".

It's an early duty, so we've got breakfast and lunch on board. Although we have the choice between a few different breakfast options, pilots can't both pick the same one in case one of us gets food poisoning. I offer first dibs to Ben, who requests a hot meal. I opt for a porridge. Lunch can be decided later, but don't get your expectations up.

Remember this is a low-cost airline, and our food will be evidence of that.

While we're offered hot drinks of our choice throughout the day at my airline, it appears that myself and Ben are both low maintenance, requiring just water today. I used to allow the cabin crew to ply me with coffee all day, every day, which is what most older captains did, but this meant I was needing to leave the flight deck for the bathroom all the time. I also started really struggling to sleep at night, so I stopped drinking caffeine at work and haven't looked back since.

I conclude the brief as I always do. "If at any point, throughout the day, any of you have any doubts, questions, concerns, or just need a break from the cabin, the flight deck door is very much open for you". Obviously, the flight deck door is actually a locked, bulletproof door that's absolutely not always open in flight, however, I think it's important for them to know that I want that line of communication to be open, and hopefully portray that Ben and I are a friendly, welcoming duo. Sometimes the cabin crew quite understandably just want a break from the passengers and being in the cabin all day, especially on longer flights, so it's nice for them to know they're welcome to take their break in the flightdeck if they wish.

A final check to see if everyone's happy or has any questions, and we're good to go. I noticed the dispatcher hanging around the main aircraft door during the latter half of my brief, indicating that he's wanting a thumbs up from us, to signal that we're ready to begin boarding. The aircraft is now due to be pushed back in 25 minutes, so I give Paul the nod and it's time to get this show on the road.

Boarding

The crew disperse to their various positions; Georgia and Ella to the back of the cabin, Ben and me into the flight deck, and John and Joel into the front galley.

I quickly plug the handwritten weight and balance figures from the load sheet into my iPad's module that I'd prepared earlier. This produces an accurate take-off weight figure along with the location of the aircraft's centre of gravity, and what trim setting we need on the rear stabiliser for take-off. While both pilots have to independently do these calculations on their respective iPads, it's PM's job to write all the outputs onto the paper load sheet, which then gets checked by PF. I leave the load sheet with my figures written onto it on the central pedestal so Ben can see it, then grab my torch and high visibility vest, announcing that "I'm going for a walkaround", slipping out just before the first passenger boards. The walkaround is PM's job, and it's essentially to check there's nothing wrong with the outside of the aircraft other than what we've already looked at in the tech log.

Although we're trusted to operate these multi-million pound machines, we're not trusted to walk around the outside of them without getting mowed down by ground vehicles, so we're required by the airport authorities to wear a high visibility vest during every walkaround. Get spotted not wearing one & you'll be reported to your airline, who will potentially take disciplinary action. While I do understand the reasoning behind it, especially at night, it just adds to the feeling that we're treated a little bit like children.

I start my walkaround at the nose of the aircraft and move around its entirety in a clockwise fashion. I'm checking the landing gear, engines, probes, wings, and all over the fuselage, looking for anything that may affect the aircraft's ability to fly or anything hanging loose that shouldn't be.

In winter, I'd also be looking for ice on the wings and fuselage. If I noticed any, we'd be required to de-ice. Thankfully it's the middle of summer so it's one less thing to think about.

While checking the aircraft over and avoiding the various servicing vehicles hurriedly driving around, I'm saying good morning to the swarm of ground staff that have descended on the aircraft. We've got two baggage belt vehicles, a water and waste truck, a fuelling truck and a tug, all currently connected to the aircraft. On top of this, there are various baggage trucks flying around with multiple trailers of bags behind them.

As I move underneath the belly of the aircraft, I notice a foot dangling out of the front cargo hold, belonging to one of the loaders who's waiting in the cargo bay for the next bags. I resist the childish temptation to tickle the back of their ankle as I scoot past.

Unfortunately, because nobody knows anybody here, I'm unsure of people's sense of humour and whether that joke would go down well, or land me in some sort of harassment legal case. Maybe one day I'll find out!

It's quite uncommon to find anything on this walkaround that's not already reported in the tech-log as we're the first flight of the day on this aircraft, so the engineers have already done their very thorough walkaround overnight. It's the down-route walkarounds that we're more likely to notice things that shouldn't be there, as we've just flown the aircraft and we're then the first person to go and look around the outside of it. Even so, mine is still a thorough one this morning, and I know there will be yet another walkaround done by one of the ground crew in 20 minutes time just before we push back.

If I do my walkaround down route, I usually re-board the aircraft from the rear steps, giving me a chance to check in with the cabin crew who are stationed down the back all day, whom I likely won't have seen since the brief at the start of the day. This morning though there's no need for that, and I can see that passengers are already starting to board from the jet bridge attached to the front door, so I don't fancy fighting the current and going the wrong way down the aircraft's single aisle to get back to the flight deck.

I walk back up to our jet bridge access door. Opening it, I find myself joining a queue of passengers all slowly shuffling towards the aircraft door. I politely ask the six or so passengers in front of me if I could squeeze past them. Boarding can be a slow process, and often, it comes to a standstill when passengers are stowing their bags. I gave up patiently waiting in this line years ago and instead now immediately request to jump the line. I've got stuff to do, and I'm sure the passengers would rather move aside than be delayed.

At this point it's usually very unclear that I'm the captain, or even a pilot for that matter. I've got a high vis vest on, but I'm also wrapped up in my black coat. I sometimes get disgruntled noises or strange looks when I ask to skip the queue, then followed by more understanding ones when they see me turn left as I board the plane rather than right.

While I've been outside, Ben's been programming the flight route into the aircraft along with various other bits of data from our flight plans using his MCDU. Much of this can be downloaded automatically now, but there are still bits we have to manually input such as selecting which runway is in use and which departure we'll fly. He's also continued the aircraft setup by turning on our Air Data Inertial Reference System (ADIRS), which is one of the many ways our aircraft will know where it is in space throughout the day. The ADIRS processes information from internal gyros and accelerometers, as well as air data inputs such as our speed, attitude and altitude to determine exactly where the aircraft is, and relays this information to the FMGCs as well as our displays in the cockpit.

I take my seat again and get busy tapping away on my own MCDU to format a message that'll be digitally sent to ATC, which is requesting clearance for our route today. As I click send, Ben takes the load sheet from the middle of the flight deck and starts inputting the data into his iPad to run his own calculations. With a steady flow of passengers now boarding, I reach up to start the Auxiliary Power Unit (APU). The APU is a very small engine located in the tail of every commercial airliner, almost invisible to anyone that doesn't know it exists.

The main purpose of the APU is to generate electricity for the aircraft when the main engines are off and the external ground power supply is disconnected. The pressurised air generated by the small engine also supplies the air conditioning on the ground and is required to start our main engines.

If you've ever been on an aircraft where the captain has mentioned they have a broken APU, then you've probably experienced what an uncomfortably warm cabin feels like, along with the extended length of time the main engine starting process takes. This is because there's no air conditioning being supplied by the APU to keep the cabin cool, and cabins get hot surprisingly fast when you cram 180 human beings into them, even when it's cold outside! There's also a very complex engine starting procedure the pilots and ground crew must follow if the APU is inoperative, so it can be a real hassle.

As our APU starts spooling up, ready to provide cool air to the passengers coming onboard, I continue the set up on my side of the flight deck. I unpack my headset from my bag & connect it to the aircraft's port above my head, stowing the headset next to me for now. Our airline does supply us with headsets, but I'd go as far as to say that they're a safety risk in themselves. They're cheap, flimsy and uncomfortable. You also need them on almost full volume to be able to understand anything, likely causing hearing damage.

The vast majority of us have chosen to invest in our own aviation-approved noise-cancelling headsets. They're expensive, at almost £1000 a set, but it's a small price to pay for something that can protect your hearing and greatly increase your comfort levels while at work all day.

Ben now places the load sheet back in between us and verbalises that his calculations agree with my work. "Weight and balance validation" he announces, which commences the next part of our set up flow. I watch and listen as Ben reads aloud the calculated zero fuel weight and centre of gravity weight figures that we've both independently calculated and agreed upon, while he's also typing them into his MCDU. With this information, the aircraft adds the fuel onboard to compute the weight at which it'll be taking off at. As the aircraft spits these figures out, Ben reads them aloud while I'm crosschecking them with my iPad figures, calling "crosschecked" to confirm that everything matches.

Next up, "Performance validation", also announced by Ben. This is the all-important stage at which we enter our take-off speeds, flap setting, and various other pieces of information that's been calculated by our iPad software. Ben reads aloud the weather and airport data he used for his calculations, and I'm checking to make sure that I've put the same data into mine. He then inserts the various outputs from the iPad into the MDCU, and therefore the aircraft's computer system. Once again, I must crosscheck this, so Ben reads them all aloud from his MCDU after punching them in, and I follow through on my iPad to check if they all match up.

As you can see, there's a lot of crosschecking involved in this process. Although it seems a very long-winded way of doing things, there are reasons that every part of this process has evolved into what it has become. There have been various incidents where planes departed using the wrong speeds, flap settings, runway intersection, or various other bits that should've been picked up and noticed at this set up stage.

The beautiful thing about having a 'just' culture (if you make a genuine mistake, you're encouraged to own up to it without fear of repercussions) is that every time there is an incident due to pilot error, it can be properly investigated. Plans and procedures can then be put in place to prevent other pilots making the same mistake. Many airlines thankfully encourage this culture, and each time an incident happens, the data is often shared, and most other airlines will look to revise their own procedures to try and prevent the same mistake happening.

Although having to crosscheck almost everything the other pilot calculates and inserts into the aircraft can be painstaking, we know we do it this way for a reason, so we just get on with it.

During the weight and balance process, I noticed our route clearance from ATC printing out, but didn't mention it as the first task took priority. As you'll see, lots of this job involved managing constant distraction, and choosing whether to continue focusing on one task, or interrupt it to do something else.

I now read out the clearance to Ben before clicking accept on my MCDU. The contents of it today match what we were expecting: a 'Novma1X' departure off runway 26L that'll take us due south from the airport after departure, down towards Brighton.

There's also a squawk code in the clearance, which I input into our transponder. This piece of equipment transmits our altitude, speed, location and various other bits of information about the aircraft to ATC both on the ground and once we're airborne. Each aircraft will be given a unique four number squawk code to help ATC differentiate between aircraft.

In case of emergency, all pilots are taught three special squawk codes that we can set on the transponder to alert ATC that we have a problem. Each of the three codes indicates a different problem. One means we've been hijacked, another means our radio communications have broken, and finally we use code 7700 for all other emergencies. Inputting any of these codes will light us up like a Christmas tree on ATC's radar screen and they'll give us their full attention.

As I'm entering the squawk code, there's a loud knock from beneath the flight deck. Ben and I both know what this is highly likely to be - the fueller has finished re-fuelling and is trying to get our attention to share the uplift quantity. The fueller has a large flipchart with numbers on it, which he shows to Ben from ground level. Ben reads the numbers aloud while I input them into the MCDU to be sent to our company. I also now have to fill in the fuelling amount, along with the engine oil quantity on board the aircraft, into our tech log. I do a quick calculation to crosscheck that the amount of fuel the fueller told us we've taken onboard matches what the aircraft is telling us is now in the tanks. This is an opportunity to spot a fuel leak or a misreading fuel gauge, neither of which are problems we want to take into the air.

After doing this, I sign my name and signature at the bottom of the tech log page, confirming that I accept responsibility for the aircraft in its current state and that all the legal paperwork is in order.

While I'm mid-signature, dispatcher Paul walks into the cockpit and stands over me, clearly wanting my attention. I invite him to start talking as I finish my scribble and begin to rip out a page from the tech log.

Each page of the tech log has multiple identical pages attached behind it. When we write on the top page, the ink transfers through onto the pages behind, giving us multiple copies for each flight. The initial page I write on will remain in the tech log, the second is bound for the dispatcher, and the third is for the engineers. We do this so if something were to happen with the aircraft on this sector and the tech log was destroyed, there would still be a record on the ground of the aircraft's state before departure. I rip out the copy that'll be remaining with Paul and place it on the central pedestal.

Paul informs me that the boarding gate is now closed, however, there are three passengers who checked in for the flight but haven't made it to the gate in time. He also tells me they have suitcases that've already been loaded into our cargo hold.

Since the disastrous Lockerbie bombing event in 1988, a regulation has been brought in prohibiting us from carrying suitcases in the cargo bay, whose owners are not present in the cabin. If the owner doesn't make it to the flight, their suitcases must be removed before departure. On that Pan Am Flight 103, a bomb was deliberately placed in a suitcase, which was checked in and loaded into the cargo bay of the Boeing 747. The owner of the suitcase then left the airport and never boarded the plane.

The bomb exploded as the aircraft flew over Scotland at 31,000ft, killing all 259 people onboard and 11 on the ground. Unfortunately, the regulation change couldn't save any of those lives, but it's nice to see that the aviation industry does learn from every incident and adapts in an effort to prevent the same tragedies from happening again.

The only exception to this rule is known as a rush bag; a bag that was either late or lost by the airline and now needs to be reunited with its owner. Rush bags go through an extra level of security check to ensure the contents are safe.

Today however, these aren't rush bags, so the ground crew will have to manually work through hundreds of bags in the cargo bay to find and remove the right ones. This can take anything from one minute to ten, depending on where the bags are.

While it's tempting in situations like this to wait an extra few minutes to see if the late passengers show up, it's simply not fair to potentially delay the hundreds of other passengers on the aircraft who've got here on time for the sake of the few that didn't.

Dispatcher Paul starts writing down these changes onto the paper load sheet. I use this time to start checking through the box, looking at the route and information that Ben has loaded into the aircraft's computer system. I'm comparing it against what's on my flight plan, and also comparing the departure loaded into the aircraft to the departure chart on my iPad. There are various speed constraints on some departures along with initial stopping altitudes that must be pre-selected into the FCU. Both PF and PM must check all of these.

I'm halfway through my deep dive into Ben's work when Paul hands me a newly amended load sheet, accounting for the three missing passengers and the weight of their baggage now removed. These are known as Last Minute Changes (LMCs) and it's highly uncommon to operate a flight where we don't have any of them.

As pilot monitoring, it's my job to plug these figure adjustments into my iPad which will give us our final weight and balance figures for departure. I quickly weigh up the priorities of tasks and figure that the sooner I complete Paul's paperwork, the sooner he can disembark and close the main aircraft door. I can continue crosschecking the box while Paul's moving the jet bridge away from the aircraft. Although these may seem like minor prioritisation decisions to be making, this one alone could save us a minute or so. If your workload management and prioritisation skills are poor, you can easily end up with a delayed flight due to a series of poor prioritisation decisions.

I write the new figures onto the paper load sheet, then show both the load sheet & my iPad to Ben, who crosschecks that the inputs and outputs are correct, confirming with a nod and smile. I now squiggle a signature under 'commander's acceptance'. This is legally signifying that I'm happy all the aircraft's holds and hatches have been searched, and that all the baggage and passengers have been loaded correctly and in accordance with the airline and manufacturers guidelines.

My personal policy tends to be that if any late passengers show up at the gate before this point, and if their bags are not off the aircraft yet, I'll ask the TCO if they can still let them on. As soon as we pass this point, however, we're going without them as it will absolutely delay the flight if we have to re-load the bags on and re-do our performance calculations for a third time.

I look up; our countdown clock is showing '-9'. We have nine minutes until we are due to be releasing the aircraft's parking brake for pushback. Technically, we can call ATC for pushback clearance at five minutes before our planned pushback time, so we tend to aim to be ready to go at '-5'.

I rip off the second page of the paper load sheet which is similar to our tech log, in that it's a copy of what's been written on the front page. I hand this, along with the tech log page to Paul, and thank him for his help today before saying our goodbyes.

I get back to looking through the final parts of Ben's programming in the FMGC. After a few seconds, cabin manager John comes into the flight deck to announce that the main aircraft door is now closed, also asking permission to close the flight deck door and lock us in for the next few hours.

Departure Brief

As soon as the cockpit door is slammed shut, I let Ben know I'm ready for his brief. Before any departure or arrival, PF will give PM an interactive brief. This used to be a very long-winded and one-sided affair, halfway through which the PM will almost certainly be daydreaming about anything more interesting.

This old style of briefing required PF to talk through every single thing we'd both just looked through in the MCDU, so it ended up being painstakingly long and mostly unnecessary. I'm elated to share that we now have a new style of briefing. It's much more to the point, only highlighting the things we really need to talk about, and also far more interactive.

Ben begins his brief by asking me if I have any questions from 'the box', i.e. all the bits I've just looked at in the MCDU. I shake my head, while expressing a "No" in a French accent just to add some flair to it. These consecutive early mornings are clearly making me delirious.

Next, he runs me through the big picture. "We're departing off runway two six left, on the Novma one x-ray departure, what do you think are the main threats?"

Great question. There are obviously a number of threats that come with launching what is essentially a very large jet powered tin can down a strip of tarmac at 150mph before flying it into the air, but in this brief we focus on any threats that may be unique or highly relevant to today. I cite busy airspace and crew tiredness as the two main ones. We'll be departing straight into the London Terminal Manoeuvring Area (TMA), one of the world's busiest and most congested areas of airspace. There are going to be plenty of other aircraft around us and within close proximity after departure, so we need to be very situationally aware. I've had a few early starts on the trot now and can definitely feel it, so it's important and relevant for me to mention this as a threat to Ben.

Ben agrees with my threat suggestions and discusses how we'll mitigate them. He explains that he'll navigate the busy airspace safely, by climbing slowly and being extra vigilant to monitor the aircraft around us on our Traffic Collision Avoidance System (TCAS). Other aircraft will show up on our display as little dots, also giving us an indication of how high they are, and whether they're climbing or descending.

He then addresses my tiredness point, explaining that to avoid mistakes, we'll take everything nice and slow, avoiding rushing. I concur. To try and further promote the open atmosphere I want to create in the cockpit, I add that if at any point in the day Ben sees me doing something he doesn't like or isn't sure about, to please speak up. I tell him I'll be doing the same the other way around. It's all about having each other's backs in here. We've both been up since before the crack of dawn so we're both going to be feeling the effects of tiredness today, and we both want the same successful outcome from the day.

Ben then moves onto what we call the 'how to' part of the brief. He runs through exactly how he's planning to operate the aircraft on the departure, so that we're both sharing the same mental model of what's about to happen.

"We're expecting a pushback off this stand to face to the south. Expecting taxi routing of Quebec, Lima, Papa, Alpha November to Alpha Two holding point. As we've got a long taxi to the runway, I'll start one engine initially and the second one once we can see how busy the holding point is. I'll fly a standard departure and put the autopilot in before thrust reduction altitude".

We're encouraged by our airline to only start one of our engines when taxiing out to the runway. As well as saving fuel and therefore our environmental impact, it also helps reduce wear and tear on the engines themselves.

We only need a warmup time of three minutes from the moment our engine starts, to the moment we can set take-off power and safely depart, so as we're expecting about a 15 minute taxi-time this morning it makes sense to only start one engine initially.

To complete the brief, Ben runs through a quick emergency brief. We are no longer required to do this daily, but if a first officer ever wants to do so, I'm certainly never going to stop them. The point of an emergency brief is to recap what our actions would be if we suffered an engine fire or failure on take-off. Although we run through these scenarios in the sim every six months, having this fresh in our minds now will be highly beneficial should we be unfortunate enough to suffer such a failure today.

Ben begins, "Up to 100 knots you can call stop for anything. Between 100 knots and V1, you can call stop for any major malfunctions. Any uninhibited ECAM warnings or cautions, or any fire or failure you deem may affect the safety of the flight. If you do call stop, what would your actions be?"

Although Ben's PF today, if we have to reject the take-off, I'll automatically assume control, so now it's over to me, "I'll call stop! I'll immediately apply full reverse on the thrust and monitor the automatic braking, taking over if necessary. I'll maintain the centreline and once the aircraft comes to a stop, I'll stow the reversers, set the parking brake and make a PA 'attention crew at stations'". This is an alert call which instructs the crew to move towards their nearest emergency exit and prepare to evacuate the aircraft. They won't do anything else until they hear my next command.

Back to Ben now "Once you call stop, I'll call spoilers, reverse green, decel, and let ATC know we're stopping. Once we've stopped, we'll catch our breath and either look at the ECAM to diagnose the issue, or use external sources such as ATC or the fire brigade to try and build a picture of what's going on and whether we need to evacuate the aircraft or not".

Superb brief from Ben so far. Clear and concise, just sharing what we need to know. Essentially, during this rejected take-off situation, as I'm focusing on slowing the aircraft down, he'll be looking inside to check that the spoilers have deployed, the engine reversers are working, and that the aircraft is decelerating.

Now, on to the next part of the brief for Ben. "If we have an engine fire or failure past V1 speed, I'll continue the take-off. I'll keep the aircraft straight on the runway centreline using the rudder until I hear you call 'rotate'. I'll then pitch the aircraft up toward 12.5 degrees, then back down to ten. As we climb away from the ground, we'll raise the landing gear and I'll start applying the rudder trim. Once the aircraft is stable and climbing away, I'll engage the autopilot. Once we're above 400ft I'll pull the heading knob to keep us flying in a straight line and ask you to confirm what the ECAM page is telling us. We'll then run through the ECAM procedure to secure the engine, and follow the 'engine-out' departure. If it's an uncontained engine fire that can't be extinguished, we'll request a right hand visual circuit from ATC and land back on runway two six left. Any questions or anything to add?"

The 'engine out' departure is an alternative departure that we'll fly if we have an engine failure on take-off. It's different at every airport and is manually programmed into the aircraft before we push back. It is designed to keep us away from any terrain but also within the vicinity of the airport, often comprising of an early turn towards an airborne hold near the runway.

It's worth mentioning what ECAM is at this point as it's been mentioned a few times during the brief. It stands for Electronic Centralized Aircraft Monitoring, and is the heart of an Airbus aircraft. The system monitors every part of the aircraft, displaying the state of hundreds of measurables to us on two ECAM screens in the centre of the cockpit. As well as displaying the aircraft's status, it produces warnings and procedures on the cockpit screens for us to follow. Overall, it helps us manage systems and respond to failures, automatically prioritising alerts, providing checklists, and reducing workload by guiding us through abnormal situations.

It's a great brief from Ben, so the only thing I have to add is more for my own sake, "The wind today is from the left. If our number one engine (left hand) is on fire, I'll turn the aircraft's nose to the left as we stop so we're facing into the wind. If engine number two is on fire, I'll stop us straight on the runway".

In 1985, a British Air Tours Boeing 737 suffered an engine fire while taking off from Manchester airport. They rejected the take-off and stopped safely on the runway. Unfortunately, the aircraft was stopped in such a position that the prevailing wind was blowing the fire from the engine towards the fuselage. This resulted in the fire spreading into the cabin faster than the passengers could evacuate, ultimately leading to a loss of 55 lives.

Since that incident, we're encouraged to consider the wind direction and if possible, stop the aircraft such that the wind would blow the flames of an engine fire away from the fuselage, buying us time rather than taking it away.

I've often thought I'd find it interesting to see whether the passengers sat just a few meters the other side of that door would be alarmed or re-assured if they could overhear the emergency brief we just shared.

I'm happy with Ben's brief and have no questions, so I reach down by my right leg to get the checklist out in anticipation of what his next words are very likely to be.

"Cockpit preparation checks please". We run through the checklist items, which are essentially checking that the aircraft is ready and safe to be pushed back off the stand, and that everything myself & Ben need to do has been completed. I read the items out loud, and Ben checks the item, then responds with the appropriate answers.

As soon as this is done, I pick up the handset from the back of the central pedestal to give my welcome onboard PA to our passengers. Just before I do, I load up the map of our entire route on my iPad which shows all the countries we'll be passing over. I also search for the destination using the weather app on my iPhone. Although we have the detailed aviation weather forecast for our destination in our flight plan, I think the passengers really just want to know whether it's sunny or not, how the rest of the day is looking, and what the temperatures are going up to. For this, the weather app is more effective, and also means I'm not switching between apps on my iPad while talking.

I tend to keep my PAs short and sweet. There's nothing worse than hearing a pilot who drones on about irrelevant things over the PA. I introduce the crew, using the names I've written down on a sheet of paper in front of me. One thing I like to do is explain the departure routing. As a passenger, if I have a window seat, I like to know where we're going to be flying over so I know what I'm looking at. As such, I always give a quick brief about where the initial few turns of the departure will be taking us over, and which areas will be visible out of each side of the aircraft. I've had multiple passengers come into the flight deck at the end of flights to express their gratitude for me taking the time to tell them, so for now I continue to do it.

After sharing flight times and the expected weather, I let them know Ben is flying the aircraft down to Alicante and that he'll get back to them once we're in the cruise with a further update. In our airline, the captain does the welcome onboard PA, and then whoever is PF will do another PA in the cruise.

As I'm putting the handset back down, Ben and I put our headsets on and hear our ground intercom crackling to life.

Slots

Before we move on, I want to touch on the topic of slots as it's something I constantly get asked about. Anyone who regularly flies on short-haul airlines will have no doubt heard the term 'slot' and likely have been impacted by one.

A slot is essentially a time given to us by air traffic control that restricts the time at which we can depart. They're usually used in busy summer periods in an attempt to manage how many aircraft are in certain areas of airspace at any one time.

There's a vast array of reasons that can cause a slot to be generated for your flight. The most common are ATC capacity and weather. Each ATC sector will only allow a certain number of aircraft through it at any one time, so the controller is able to safely manage the flow of traffic without being overloaded. Across Europe, ATC often have staffing issues due to sickness or strikes (more often than not, it's the French). During these times, the capacity of each sector is greatly reduced, meaning that any flights operating through that sector will likely have a delaying slot placed on them.

When weather is involved, it's a similar story. Aircraft will need to divert around severe weather, often spilling out into surrounding ATC sectors and all wanting to take a similar routing to avoid the weather. To keep things safe, ATC will reduce the number of aircraft flying on a routing that takes them near the weather, so that the increased workload for the controllers will remain manageable. Although slots can be frustrating, more often than not they're there to keep things safe.

What can we do as pilots when we get a slot? The first thing we can do is send ATC what's known as a 'ready message'. We can only do this once everyone's onboard, the aircraft door is closed and we're all ready to be pushed back. Once this message is sent, ATC will try their best to give us any improvements on the current slot time. If someone in front of us misses their slot, we're in prime position to take it.

Another thing we can do is request remote holding, whereby we push back off our parking stand at our original departure time, even when we have a delaying slot. We'll then taxi the aircraft to a holding point closer to the runway and shut our engines down again. The main benefit of this is that when it's approaching our slot time, we can just start our engines and go. We don't need to rely on the ground crew to come and push us back. During busy summer periods, tugs can be a precious resource even at major airports. Remote holding frees them up for everyone else, while decreasing our reliance on them to be there at the exact time we'd need them. Thankfully today, there's no slot, so it's straight into the normal pushback procedure.

Pushback

"Flight deck from ground. Hello sir, we've completed our ground checks and we're ready to push your aircraft back". While PM is in charge of the majority of the communication, PF is in charge of communicating with the ground crew. That voice is from one of our tug team who'll be pushing the aircraft back. They're talking to us via a headset they've attached to a port in our nose wheel bay.

Ben speaks to the ground crew through the intercom, and this is my cue to request pushback clearance from ATC's ground frequency. It's a busy frequency with various other aircraft asking for pushback or taxi instructions. Each lengthy instruction has to be read back afterwards too, so you can often end up waiting a substantial amount of time before you can transmit your request. It's a skill in itself being able to time your radio transmission without 'stepping on' someone else. This is when two aircraft start transmitting at exactly the same time, which essentially blocks the radio, and nobody can hear what either is saying. When you transmit on the radio, you can't hear if anyone else is simultaneously transmitting, so this happens a surprising amount.

I find an opportune moment to sneak in a pushback clearance request, which is quickly approved. Ben turns the flashing red beacon light on to indicate to everyone around us that the aircraft is about to start moving. I switch our transponder on, with our squawk code already pre-set, so ATC can now see us on their radar screen as we move around the airport. We run our 'before start' checklist, and then Ben tells the ground crew we're ready to move. They instruct him to release the parking brake, and with a small jolt as the tug starts pushing the aircraft backwards, we're away!

A glance up at the timing screen which shows '-2'. It's not '-5', but it'll do! It'll go down as an on time departure.

This is a good time in the book to discuss the controversial topic of looking at flight plans and setting up all my iPad modules before I'm technically at work. Especially given that our unions claim we should only start looking at anything work related after we've reported for duty and are therefore getting paid for our time.

Well, hopefully you've now built an understanding of just how tight we are on time from the moment we arrive at work to when we need to pushback. This is on a good day, where nothing's gone wrong.

From the moment I step foot onto the aircraft, there's constantly something or someone needing my attention. Now, if we throw into the mix a technical or passenger issue that requires me to pause the normal procedures while I deal with it, you can see how we'd easily end up departing late.

I like to think it's just good airmanship to have everything as prepared as it can be and already starting to build my situational awareness for the day before stepping foot onto the aircraft.

There are a number of examples where I've spotted something in the flight plan or aircraft defects while on my walk from the car park to the terminal that would result in us being unable to dispatch the aircraft that day.

One of which was just a few weeks ago; I noticed a Flight Control Unit (FCU) fault noted in the aircraft defects list. While this usually isn't a big issue as we have two FCUs, and are able to dispatch the aircraft with just one, a quick read into the limitations of flying with just one told me we couldn't make an approach to a runway using a landing system we call 'RNP'.

The fact we couldn't do an RNP approach also wouldn't usually be an issue as most airports offer various types of approach, and our base airport usually has an Instrument Landing System (ILS) onto their main runway, a type of approach that we can indeed do with this aircraft today even with the FCU fault.

In the name of keeping the technical things relatively light, I won't go any deeper into these different types of approaches, but if you wish to find out more, please check out the blog piece on approach types found at PilotBible.com.

The thought process for some people may stop here, satisfied that the fault shouldn't impact the day, as after all, the airline is aware of this defect and have still given us this aircraft to operate this route today. Someone with good airmanship, however, will continue to dig until they're completely 100% sure.

Continuing through the flight plan to the NOTAMs section, I noticed that our base airport was planning to close their main runway that evening, before we'd be getting back. They were planning on switching to their smaller runway, which doesn't have an ILS and only has an RNP approach. Cogs started turning rapidly in my head.

The only other type of approach I'm aware of that we could do would be a 'visual' approach, where we essentially conduct the approach by looking out the window at the runway. Again, this usually would be fine and more than doable. A quick look at the weather forecast in the flight plan, however, showed me that there was overcast low cloud forecast all night, which means we simply wouldn't be legally able to start a visual approach as we wouldn't be able to see the runway.

While still on the walk in, I phoned the control tower from my personal phone, explained the dilemma to them and asked if they could think of any solutions. They confirmed that the only approach they could offer us would be either an RNP or a visual, neither of which we could do.

It clicked into place, that due to all these issues lining up in a very unfortunate way, if we dispatched the aircraft that day, we wouldn't be able to land it back into London that evening.

I then called our operations department to run them through my line of thinking, which they agreed with, and told me they'd call me back. By the time I was through security, our ops department had already swapped us onto a different aircraft, located on the other side of the airport.

In this example, if I'd only opened the flight plans once I was onboard the aircraft, amongst all the other distractions taking place & having to set the aircraft up, go for the walkaround etc, it would have taken me a lot longer to come to the same conclusion, by which time we may already have boarded the passengers and then found ourselves in a very sticky situation where we'd have a plane full of passengers that aren't going anywhere. An even worse outcome could have been that due to rushing and various other bits going on as soon as I boarded the aircraft, we may have actually missed the full implications of the issue, only realising later that night when we approached London that we actually weren't able to land at our base.

You may now be thinking well why don't you look at all this stuff at home before leaving for work in a more relaxed environment, rather than doing it while trying to navigate next to main roads and through terminals at the same time? That would be a fair question.

I believe there's a balance to find here. For me, disrupting my sleep to an even greater extent than it already is, to sit and look at flight plans before I leave the house, isn't a sacrifice that's sensible in my eyes, nor is it expected.

If I'm on late duties, I'll usually take a look at the flight plans before leaving the house late morning, as I'll be up anyway, but on earlies I need all the sleep I can get to be as alert as I can be during the duty.

Back to the situation at hand. As we're being pushed backwards, Ben commences the engine start procedure. He points to the ignition switch next to the thrust levers on the central pedestal and calls out "Ignition". I look down to check he's pointing at the correct thing. Although this procedure may seem like overkill, the engine ignition switch is very close to the parking brake handle & they both move in the same manner.

There have been occurrences across the industry of tired pilots switching the parking brake on during pushback in this Airbus fleet, when they intended to turn the engine ignition switch on. These are known as 'slips', where you intend to do one thing but mistakenly and unintentionally do another. This particular slip has resulted in injuries to the tug drivers and crew on board, so this part of the engine start procedure now has to be crosschecked by both pilots before anything is moved.

Ben switches on the ignition, before moving the master switch for Engine 1 to ON. Slowly but surely, we hear the gentle rumble of the left-hand engine grow louder as high-pressure air supplied from the APU starts turning the main engine fan blades, and then the turbine blades. Eventually, fuel is released into the engine and ignited, causing the engine to 'light up'.

Although this whole process is managed automatically by our aircraft's incredibly clever engine computer system known as Full Authority Digital Engine Control (FADEC), we're still expected to monitor the engine parameters during start up.

It's a successful start on engine one. As we're planning to taxi on just a single engine initially, Ben begins his 'after start' flow, turning the ignition switch off and prodding a few buttons on the overhead panel. After monitoring him as he runs his flow, I commence my flow under Ben's watchful eyes this time. I arm our ground spoilers, so they'll deploy if we reject the take-off. I extend the flaps to our take-off position and set the trim wheel for take-off using the figure we calculated in our weight and balance calculations.

We used to do these flows simultaneously, until once again people started missing bits or pushing the wrong buttons. Now they're monitored flows, so one pilot watches while the other does, then vice versa.

The aircraft comes to a smooth stop on the taxiway and Ben sets the parking brake under the instruction of the ground crew, before thanking them for their help and dispatching them. They disconnect their tug, headset, and a pin they used to disconnect the nose wheel steering from our flight deck controls during the pushback sequence.

The tug and ground crew clear the aircraft to the left-hand side, giving us a goodbye wave once they're clear. During this wave they're also required to show us the pin, so we know they've removed it. If they didn't, we'd soon have an embarrassing moment when we approach the first corner ahead of us on the taxiway and find out we're unable to turn the aircraft!

Taxi

The departure of the ground crew is my cue to call ATC and request our taxi clearance. The ground frequency has been full of constant chatter since we last spoke to them, so again it's a waiting game to get a word in edgeways. When I finally do, we're given our taxi clearance to the runway. Every taxiway is marked with a letter, displayed on large signs adjacent to the taxiway and also on the tarmac itself. These letters match up to the taxiway chart we now have up next to us on our iPads.

Our clearance today is delivered as Ben briefed earlier; "Quebec, Lima, Papa, Alpha November to Alpha Two holding point". This essentially means, taxi on the taxiway marked as Q, then onto the one marked as L, then P, then AN, and stop at A2. A2 being the holding point just before the runway. Ben flicks the taxi light on, and after we both check that our respective sides of the aircraft are clear of vehicles and people, he releases the park brake and puts thrust onto the left engine to start us rolling forward.

As we approach our first turn, Ben's right hand is resting on what's known as a tiller. It's a small handle located behind his sidestick which controls the direction of our nosewheel in order to turn the aircraft on the ground. He rotates this to the left to turn us onto taxiway L and releases the pressure on it once the nosewheel is on the centreline.

As we make our next turn, we can see that there are a number of aircraft already queuing at the A2 holding point. Seven to be precise, which means we're going to be waiting there a while. There's a minimum distance and amount of time that must be left between aircraft taking off or landing, which vary depending on the size of each aircraft. These gaps are mandatory to protect us from the potential lethal effects of wake turbulence.

When an aircraft's wing travels through the air, it leaves a trail of disrupted air behind it. This unsettled air tends to spiral into vortices (there are many videos on YouTube of aircraft flying through fog or cloud where the vortices can be very clearly seen). If another aircraft flies through this unsettled air that's spinning around, it's almost certainly going to have an adverse effect on the controllability of that aircraft, potentially even leading to an uncontrollable state. The bigger and heavier the aircraft, the larger and more powerful the vortices caused by it are, so the longer the gap required behind it.

Today, most of the aircraft at the holding point are of a similar size to ours, which only require a two minute gap between aircraft taking off. With seven other aircraft already at the holding point, I know it's going to be at least 15 minutes until it's our turn to depart. If we then add into the mix that there will be aircraft intermittently landing between the seven aircraft departing ahead of us, we're already looking at a 20-25 minute wait at the holding point. It was a good call from Ben to only start one engine!

This extended wait at the holding point has unfortunately become the normal here at this big London base. I've spent a considerable part of my life sitting at holding point A2. I'd actually be a bit scared to calculate just how many cumulative hours of my life I've spent queuing at that holding point. One benefit of being sat there, however, is that we get the best seat in the house to spectate on the stream of inbound aircraft landing, and yes, as pilots we do sit there and judge our colleagues' touchdowns.

We taxi up to the back of the aircraft in front of us and Ben sets the parking brake. I make a quick PA to update our passengers on our position in the queue and the expected wait time. This is not mandatory, but I try and put myself in their shoes. They can only see left and right out the aircraft, and not the large queue in front of us. I like to keep them informed and manage their expectations so they're not sitting there wondering why we've been sat stationary for so long. Being in the know can also help settle the anxiety of any nervous flyers on board.

At this point, Ben and I don't have too much to do as we can't run our next checklist until we've started the next engine. We spend the next ten minutes running through any of the standard small talk questions I referred to earlier that haven't already been asked; Where do you live? How's the drive in from there? I then move onto trying to find out what we have in common to talk about for the rest of the day.

We slowly creep forward in the queue as we chat, watching our fellow colleagues depart and land in a sequence that's timed down to the second. We watch and listen as an aircraft from another company, five in front of us in the departure queue, is given clearance to line up on the runway and is told to be "ready immediately" by ATC. This means the controller is trying to squeeze them into a small gap between the aircraft that's just landed, and the next one that's about to land. In order to make this efficient plan work successfully, the departing aircraft needs to start their take-off roll the second the controller clears them for take-off. Engines on airliners can take up to eight seconds to spool up from idle to take-off power, so in situations like this we tend to advance the thrust levers towards take-off power before the controller has even finished that transmission clearing us for take-off.

Although we hear the pilot acknowledge the clearance to be ready immediately, Ben and I both know that the foreign airline just lining up are notorious for causing issues at this airport. The controller then asks the British Airways Boeing 777, which is on its final approach, to slow down to its minimum approach speed and expect a late landing clearance. Technically, a landing clearance can come at any point before the wheels touch down, but realistically you don't want to be initiating a go-around due to no landing clearance very close to the ground as it's leaving less room for error.

We both lean forwards slightly in our seats to watch the show unfold, while still discussing our subjects of interest. The departing aircraft is cleared for an immediate take-off, but the lack of urgency in the pilot's readback of the clearance, along with the fact that five seconds later there's still no sign of the aircraft moving forwards, indicates this situation is about to get spicy.

The controller makes another, more direct and authoritative sounding order for the aircraft to begin its take-off roll immediately. The pilot doesn't respond, but we can see the heat distortion in the air behind the engines starting to grow larger, meaning the pilots are just starting to apply power to the engines. We can see the BA 777 on approach getting ever closer, and excited noises start coming from both sides of our cockpit at what we might be about to watch. We know exactly what the crew of the 777 are thinking. They'll be running through their go-around actions and preparing as best they can in case they have to abort this landing, while probably also already cursing the slow moving traffic on the runway.

The aircraft on the runway trundles past our right hand window. Eventually, we lose sight of it as it continues to gain speed while rolling down the runway. However, the 777 is now just two hundred feet off the ground, a few seconds from touchdown. "Speedbird 551, go around, I repeat, go-around". The order from ATC is delivered with urgency and clarity over the radio.

I get a surge of adrenaline even hearing the call, let alone being the one to receive it. Ben and I let out even more excitable noises knowing that we've got front row seats to watch the 777 conduct a standard, but relatively rare manoeuvre. The nose of the 777 rapidly pitches up. Simultaneously, plumes of grey smoke blast out the back of its engines as the pilot pushes the throttles up to full power. It's a few seconds before the thrust kicks in, and the aircraft then climbs steeply away from the runway as the landing gear doors open to allow the wheels to retract. I know how hard the pilots are currently working in there and do feel sorry for them, especially as they've likely just flown through the night to get here, but they're giving us an exciting show nonetheless. Only now does the 777 read back their go-around instruction, but they've done what any good pilots do: Aviate, Navigate and then Communicate, in that order. Actioning the go-around and ensuring the aircraft is climbing away safely is far more important than reading back the ATC instruction. The tower can see what they're doing anyway, so acknowledging the instruction isn't high up on their priorities. ATC then instruct the 777 to conduct an immediate left turn during their go around, as the current scenario could lead to what's known as a 'piggyback' event; the aircraft that was slow to take-off is now airborne and ascending towards the 777 which is directly above it. None of the pilots will be able to see the other aircraft directly below or above them, which is a highly unsettling feeling, so peeling the 777 off to the left and letting the departing aircraft continue straight ahead prevents this situation.

ATC then transfer the 777 back over the radar controller frequency, where they'll be re-sequenced into the landing pattern. The BA crew remain professional over the radio and avoid dropping any expletives aimed at the aircraft that didn't obey ATC's instructions, although I'm sure within their flight deck it's a different story.

With the exciting show over, our focus returns to our own flight deck. We decide to start engine number two as there's now only four aircraft left to depart in front of us. This time, I start the engine, as Ben's priority as PF is to keep his eyes outside and control the plane, not be fiddling with any switches or levers inside. I still have to confirm the ignition switch with him, and two minutes later our engine 2 is all fired up.

I start a stopwatch timer on the aircraft so we'll be able to check we've had our three minute engine warm up period before we depart, then run my hands across another flow in the flight deck, turning the ignition off, the APU off as we no longer need it, and opening up the 'status' page on our ECAM screen to check if any defects have been noticed by the aircraft between when we pushed back and now.

We run our 'after start' checklist, followed by conducting our flight control checks. From the cockpit windows, we can only see the tips of our wings, so we use our ECAM system display screen to check that moving the flight controls in the cockpit correlates with the correct control surfaces moving on the wings and tail.

Halfway through these checks, a loud buzzer rings in the cockpit. I look down to see it's the cabin crew trying to call us. I'm 99% sure what the call from the cabin crew will be, so I prioritise finishing the last few seconds of the flight control check to prevent us having to start it all over again. "Your radios," I say to Ben, indicating he is now responsible for monitoring and responding to ATC while I speak to the cabin crew over our interphone channel. This is still done through our headsets by simply selecting a button on the audio control panel just below the MCDU.

Cabin manager John is on the other end of the phone, confirming that the cabin is secured for take-off. I turn over a plastic flipper in the flight deck, flipping it from 'secured for landing' to 'secured for take-off', then thank John before ending the call and taking the radio's back off Ben.

I then run through another flow, switching on the weather radar which radiates out the front of the aircraft and can be damaging to any humans standing on the ground directly in front of it, so we only turn it on at this stage once we're clear of any parking areas. I check the transponder, ensuring it's set for take-off, and arm our maximum level of autobrake which will kick in along with the spoilers should we need to reject the take-off.

Finally, I press a button on the ECAM Control Panel (ECP) which tells the aircraft we're about to take-off. If it detects that something is not set up correctly for take-off, such as the flaps not set, it's going to start making some very loud noises. No loud noises come our way, so Ben asks me to complete a PEDS brief, which is the next stage of our procedure. It stands for Performance, Engine-Out, Departure, Stop Altitude. This brief consists of me running through a big picture verbalisation of our departure and crosschecking it with the clearances we've written down.

"Performance, we're taking off from runway two six left from intersection alpha two, we calculated using figures from intersection bravo, so we have performance in hand. The engine-out procedure for this runway is to climb straight ahead to 1700ft, then make a left turn. Departure, we're cleared for a Novma one x-ray departure, which is crosschecked here on our ATC clearance, it's in the FMGC, and it's on my iPad chart. Stop altitude for this SID is 4,000ft on my chart, and 4,000ft is pre-set on the FCU".

Seems long-winded, crosschecking all this stuff that we've already crosschecked? I agree. But again, there's reason for it. After reading reports of crews taking off from wrong runway intersections or climbing to wrong altitudes on their departure, I've definitely come to just accept that these over the top procedures are just another way to help save us getting into trouble, even if they do feel patronisingly repetitive.

Ben calls for the taxi checklist which confirms that I've done everything correctly in my previous flow, and that the aircraft is all set up to depart.

A few more minutes of small talk later and it's our turn to go. ATC gives us our line-up clearance and as we roll onto the runway, we're completing our final flow; Ben turns the strobe lights on, as I turn our air conditioning packs off (which provides the engines with more take-off power as no air is being directed from the engines to the air conditioning system) and change the mode on our transponder yet again.

The 'line up checklist' requested by Ben is then read by me and responded to by him, while he's also turning the aircraft onto the centreline of the runway and bringing us to a stop. Multitasking at its finest!

Departure

We sit stationary on the runway for a few seconds while waiting for our next clearance. It's always a strange feeling, staring down one of the world's busiest runways, completely stationary. The sun is now rising over my left hand shoulder, producing an array of colours in the sky, overhead the 2500 meters of runway stretching off into the distance in front of us.

I use this time to look at the windsock that's located to the side of the runway and run through in my head again which way I'd turn the aircraft if we had an engine fire and had to abort the take-off.

We then receive our take-off clearance. Ben advances the thrust levers up to 50% power as I readback the clearance to ATC. We allow the engines to settle at 50% before applying full power. It's a way for us to check that all the parameters are stable, but also negates the problem of one engine spooling up much faster than the other. All engines are slightly different; some are newer, and some are a little older. One of our engines is obviously warmer than the other as it's been running for longer, and one's also got more airflow coming through it as it's on the into wind. All of these things can mean one engine is a little faster than the other when going from idle to full power. If you slam the throttles straight from idle to full power and one engine spooled straight up while the other took a few seconds longer, the aircraft would be put into an uncontrollable turn, and you'd likely end up on the grass off the side of the runway. At 50% thrust, it's not really enough power to turn the aircraft too much, but enough to get both engines ready to accelerate to full power simultaneously.

Sure enough, today our right hand engine takes a few seconds longer than the left to reach 50%. Once they're both settled nicely at 50%, Ben pushes the levers forward into the take-off detent, and we're slowly pressed into the back of our seat by the force of the forward acceleration. He announces the various modes that are now displaying on his Primary Flight Display (PFD – one of the two main screens in front of him) and his calls are checked by me.

He takes his hand off the thrust levers and it's replaced by mine. Although Ben is PF and is steering the aircraft down the centreline with his foot pedals, it's the captain's decision whether to abort a take-off. If I decide to abort, I immediately assume control of the aircraft from Ben and my first action will be to pull the thrust levers into full reverse, so my hand remains primed and ready on them.

As we gain speed down the runway, now passing through 50kts, I'm monitoring our engine parameters, checking for any abnormalities. Ben's job as PF is to keep his eyes outside, looking for anything that may affect our take-off; vehicles crossing the runway, birds, etc. As captain, in between monitoring the engine parameters, I'm also glancing outside from time to time, while also intermittently looking at Ben and also all of our other instruments. This requires a rapid scan, moving my eyes and attention from one thing to the next very quickly, and it's a way of ensuring that I'm aware of as much as possible during the take-off roll.

As Ben briefed, up to 100kts I can call 'stop' for almost anything. It's much safer to reject a take-off below this speed than continue with an issue that we're unsure about. Above 100kts, however, a rejected take-off becomes a more dangerous procedure. Decelerating a 70 tonne aircraft from high speed to a stop in a matter of seconds takes a huge amount of braking power. This inevitably leads to extremely hot brakes and tyres, which brings with it an array of other risks such as fires or bursting tyres.

As such, up to 100kts I'm 'stop minded'. Looking around the flight deck for anything that may make me decide that it's best to abort this take-off. At 100kts, I call the speed out, to which Ben calls 'checked'. We're checking that our instruments are aligned with each other, and it's also a way to check that the other pilot isn't incapacitated.

We're now accelerating rapidly beyond 100kts, being pushed deeper into the back of our seats. I alter my hand position ever so slightly on the thrust lever, dropping it slightly down and backwards, to remind myself that unless a small list of really bad things go wrong between now and liftoff, taking the problem into the air will most likely be the safest option.

Our speed is now quickly approaching V1, the speed after which we'll not reject the take-off for anything. Even if we have an engine failure while still on the runway but above V1, it's safer to continue the take-off on one engine, as there may not be enough runway left to bring the aircraft to a stop without ploughing off the end of it. Our iPad software calculated this speed earlier in the day.

One thing I often think about at this point is the following: An engine failure is indicated by a bang and a yawing motion to one side. If this happens just before V1, I'd need to reject the take-off.

Another issue that is also indicated by a bang and a yawing motion to one side would be one of our main tyres bursting. If we have a tyre burst as we're approaching V1, the braking ability on that side is greatly reduced and it's therefore much more preferable to continue the take-off and return for a landing where we'd have the entirety of the runway to stop the aircraft, rather than the tiny bit that's now left in front of us.

We've practiced both these scenarios in the simulator and the initial symptoms feel extremely similar from within the cockpit. The issue in real life is that I could have just a split second to diagnose whether we have an engine issue or a tyre issue, and then either abort the take-off or push the thrust levers forward to their maximum power position to get us off the ground sooner, depending on what I believed had happened. If I got the split second diagnosis wrong, it could lead to a very messy scenario indeed. It's a position I hope never to be in, but it is important to consider nonetheless.

Today we hurtle through V1 without any bangs. As we do, I lift my hand off the thrust levers and call "V1". This is it. No stopping for anything now. A few seconds later I call "rotate". The speed's passing 142 kts, which again was calculated by our software as the speed at which Ben must pull back on his sidestick and lift the front wheel off the ground.

We're now pushed downwards into our seat as the front of the aircraft is rotated into the air. As the nose pitches up, the horizon gets lower and lower in our field of view. Ben, I, and all our passengers are now aiming at the sky.

We feel our main landing gear leave the ground as the wings generate enough lift to suspend 70 tonnes of aircraft in the air, something I still find absolutely mind-blowing.

During the rotation, I'm looking outside at the horizon so I can judge the rate at which ben lifts the nose. If he lifts it too quickly, there's a risk of hitting the aircraft's tail on the runway. Too slow, and there's a risk we'll travel much further down the runway than we'd like to and end up low on our departure path.

As the Airbus doesn't have control feedback into the sidesticks, I can't 'feel' what Ben's doing with his sidestick through mine. My sidestick is completely stationary as he manipulates the flight controls using his, so it's imperative I keep my eyes outside so I can judge the speed of his rotation, ready to push my take-over button on my sidestick and assume control if needs be. Once satisfied that Ben's nailed the rotation rate, I bring my gaze back into the cockpit.

I scan our instruments, now looking at our vertical speed indicator to check that it's showing a rate of climb. I double check this by confirming that our altitude according to our altimeter is also increasing. With both of these checked, I call "positive climb" to which Ben responds, "gear up".

I reach forward and grab the landing gear lever that's conveniently shaped like a wheel. Airbus specifically designed various parts of the cockpit to relate to the part of the aircraft that the lever or control operates, in an effort to help reduce pilot errors, specifically the 'slips' that I mentioned earlier.

I pause for a second with my hand on the gear lever as I state "gear". This procedure of calling and then pausing with my hand on the control, mandatory within our company, is giving Ben a chance to correct my mistake if I've grabbed the wrong control. Ben doesn't slap my hand off the lever, so a second later, I call "up" while simultaneously raising the lever.

The thuds and bangs below our feet indicate the gear doors are opening to allow the landing gear to retract into the fuselage. We feel heavy vibrations as the nosewheel is lifted into its bay while still rotating, and feel the vibrations gradually diminish as the spinning wheel comes to a stop. For the first time since we applied take-off power, everything now feels smooth. I have a quick scan of the instruments, and everything looks good. We're climbing away from the ground nicely at the expected speed and pitch attitude.

Without the gear, the aircraft becomes a lot more aerodynamic. There's just one more thing we need to do to make it as aerodynamic as possible, retract the flaps. They were there to help us get off the ground as quickly as possible, but we no longer need them extended. As we pass 1,000ft, Ben pitches the nose down a few degrees to begin the acceleration phase of our departure.

So far, we've been climbing away from the ground at V2 speed. At around 150kts, it's a speed designed to give us a good rate of climb away from the ground but not much use if we want to get all the way down to Spain today. At some stage we need to transition into faster forward flight, and that's now.

When departing any airport, we usually climb away from the runway initially at a steep angle, with full take-off thrust applied, and keeping the aircraft's speed constant at V2. For a standard departure, we maintain this until we reach 1,000ft above the airport. Once at this altitude, known as our 'acceleration altitude', we begin the transition to a more efficient flying speed. Some airports that are very close to large cities may incorporate a more restrictive noise abatement procedure into their departure, whereby the 1,000ft acceleration altitude gets moved up to 3,000ft above ground level. This essentially means that aircraft will be much higher by the time they're over the city, reducing noise pollution for residents and increasing safety margin in terms of height should something go wrong over the built-up area.

As Ben lowers the nose, he simultaneously reduces the thrust on the engines. We no longer need the take-off thrust setting that was required to get us off the ground, and we can save some wear and tear as well as fuel by climbing away with a lower amount of thrust.

Our airspeed begins to increase, and just as it approaches the speed at which our flaps need to be retracted, ATC transmit an instruction for us to transfer over to London's frequency, a message that needs to be readback by me.

The aircraft's speed is increasing fast, so again it's a split second prioritisation decision. Do I respond to ATC which may delay the flap retraction, or do I ignore them for a few seconds and focus on retracting the flaps? Jumping back to our Aviate, Navigate, Communicate framework, I hold off responding to the ATC call as Ben calls "Flaps 0". I crosscheck that our airspeed is still increasing, and we are above the minimum safe speed to retract the flaps. I confirm this by calling "speed checked", then similarly to the gear procedure, I place my hand on the flap lever and call out "flaps", waiting a further second before moving it. I watch on our systems display screen as both the flaps and slats symbols on the wing retract until the 1 turns to a 0, then I call "0".

In the same breath I respond to ATC's call, squeezing the red trigger on the back of my sidestick with my index finger to transmit as I talk. I reach down and flick over the frequencies on the Radio Control Panel next to my right leg. The frequency we can expect to be changed onto can often be found on our departure chart. It's not procedure to pre-select the frequency before departure, but it's another example of how we can buy some time by anticipating and thinking ahead. I dialled in this London frequency to our standby channel while we were sat stationary waiting in the take-off queue, so instead of having my head down right now fiddling with the radio tuner knob, I simply click a button to transfer our standby frequency to the active one.

The London frequency is as chaotic as we'd expect at this time in the morning. Non-stop chatter with aircraft checking in, checking out, being informed of holding and delays over London and controllers dealing with various other requests. I try to check in with them when I hear the first second of silence, but my transmission gets stepped on by another aircraft. Ben engages the autopilot by pressing a button on the FCU and calls "Autopilot 2" as he confirms on his PFD that it's successfully engaged. Although he'll now use the knobs on the FCU to manipulate the autopilot and control the aircraft, his right hand remains on his sidestick, as mine has been since take-off. Various things may cause the autopilot to drop out or disengage, and when we're still this close to the ground, it's good airmanship to have the manual controls covered.

It's another 30 seconds before I can get a word in edgeways on the radio, by which point we're already levelling off at our initially cleared altitude. During that time, I finish my after-take-off flow by retracting the landing lights and disarming the ground spoilers. I finally manage to check in with London, who clear us up to flight level 80 and instruct us to continue on our SID. Ben controls the autopilot by dialling in '8,000' into the FCU altitude window and pulls the knob which puts the aircraft into a climb.

If ATC had cleared us to an 'altitude', we could climb up to 8,000ft. As they cleared us to a 'flight level', we have to change the pressure setting on our altimeter, otherwise known as QNH. Flight levels are based on all aircraft using the same pressure setting to ensure safe and accurate vertical separation between aircraft. This setting is 1013hpa, otherwise known as 'STD' on the Airbus. Ben and I both pull our QNH knobs to change our altimeter settings to STD, and Ben calls out the flight level now being displayed.

As we're doing this, we notice another aircraft on our Traffic Collision Avoidance System (TCAS). The small blip that's just appeared on our navigation display shows another aircraft 5,000 feet above us, at flight level 90. Although we'll stop our ascent 1,000ft below them, our TCAS system doesn't take this into account, instead it looks at our current trajectory and determines if there's a risk of collision.

If the system believes we're on a crash course with just a few seconds to spare, it will order both aircraft to manoeuvre away from each other, an instruction which we must adhere to and one that takes priority over what ATC tell us to do. Our newer aircraft will actually complete the TCAS avoidance manoeuvre without any input from the pilots.

In congested airspace such as London, setting off someone's TCAS system could cause carnage. An avoidance manoeuvre from one aircraft may put that aircraft straight into the path of another, setting off a string of aircraft performing avoidance manoeuvres. ATC, meanwhile, will have a load of aircraft under their control that are doing the opposite of what they're telling them to do, as the pilots will have to comply with the TCAS orders rather than ATC's.

With our current high rate of climb, we're likely to trigger the TCAS system if we don't intervene here. Ben notices the danger presented by our high rate of ascent too, and sets '1,500' in the vertical airspeed window, pulling the knob to engage the mode as he does. This instructs the autopilot to give us a climb rate of just 1,500 feet per minute, which is much more sensible than the 3,000 feet per minute that our aircraft is currently doing.

Happy that we're no longer on a collision course with the aircraft above us, the flying conditions on the climb out seem smooth so we decide to release the cabin crew to start performing their duties. This is done by switching the seatbelt sign off and back on quickly, making a double chime noise in the cabin, which is their cue that we're happy for them to move around. If we were flying in poor weather or anticipating any bumps on the rest of the departure, we'd delay this action until we can find smooth air.

I now reach forward and switch on our Controller-Pilot Data Link Communications (CPDLC) screen. It's a relatively new bit of kit for us, and essentially, it's a digital communication system that enables ATC to communicate with us via text instead of voice. It's a great way to free up the busy airwaves. I log onto London's network, then get a message notifying us that we're connected. Almost immediately, I get another notification that London wants us to climb to FL290. I can see that Ben's looking at the clearance on my screen, so I don't bother reading it out loud, but silently confirm with London that we accept the request using a button on the panel.

Once we get a notification that London has received our acceptance, Ben dials in FL290 into the FCU. As the nose pitches up to continue ascending away from the earth, the auto thrust piles on the power to hold the aircraft's speed steady at 250kts.

Things are getting a little quieter in the cockpit now. Although the radios are still busy with non-stop chatter, the workload our end is dying down. It gives us a little bit of time to enjoy the views out the window. I look down at Brighton to my left as the sun continues to rise over the English Channel. It's 6 am, and I think to myself that the majority of people down there are likely still tucked up in bed fast asleep. While the view I have right now is pretty spectacular, I'd be lying if I didn't feel a pang of jealousy towards those getting their full eight hours of sleep.

Passing through FL100, it's our cue to commence more action in the flight deck. I take a look inside at the calculated landing time on the MCDU, and compare it to our scheduled landing time. Due to the slot and departure queue out of London, we're planned to arrive ten minutes late into Alicante. I'm confident we can make this time up through various means in the cruise. So far, the aircraft has been travelling at a maximum speed of 250kts, which is the speed limit for all aircraft below FL100. Above FL100 the limit no longer applies, and our clever aircraft knows this. The magenta speed indicator on our PFD jumps from 250kts to 280kts and the aircraft simultaneously pitches down to accelerate towards the new speed target, before pitching up to continue the climb.

Ben and I also now have a few more tasks to do. Ben deletes the engine-out flight plan from the box and removes various other bits of data that we no longer need in there. We both change a few settings on our navigation display to show us the nearest airports. That's now more valuable than showing the height and speed constraints of the departure we've just completed. In the Airbus, you can see either, but not simultaneously.

I use the electric switch on the right of my seat to move it back and recline it slightly, a sure sign that things are going swimmingly. This position is a bit more relaxed and comfortable than the upright position we sit in for take-off and landing. As I do, I ask Ben if he's happy with the seatbelts being turned off. We're above FL100 now and it seems nice and smooth. After a nod from Ben, my right hand reaches up to switch off the signs, as my left hand undoes my own seatbelt shoulder straps.

In the Airbus, we have a five-point harness consisting of two shoulder straps, two lap straps, and a strap between our legs. These straps would keep us securely in our seats in a rejected take-off or forced landing situation. Above FL100, however, the shoulder straps aren't of much use and can feel restrictive, so we're free to undo them. However, we always keep the lap straps fastened while we're seated.

During the next 15 minutes, the workload is relatively low while the aircraft climbs up to cruising altitude. There are a few frequency changes for me to make, and we're eventually transferred from London airspace into French airspace. Aside from that, further small talk has led to Ben and I realising we both have common ground in following Formula One, so we end up engrossed in conversation regarding next year's driver lineup. The aircraft occasionally makes gentle turns as we overfly waypoints. Ben programmed in these waypoints at the start of the day, and the plane is quite literally just flying from one to the next.

Cruising

As the aircraft finally levels off at FL380, it's time to start our next round of tasks. As PM, I'm responsible for crosschecking our expected flight time and fuel figures from the flight plan to see what we've actually done. It's a way of catching any fuel leaks or other significant discrepancies. As I'm doing this, Ben alters our TCAS system to look for aircraft below us rather than above, as that's more likely where a threat will come from at this altitude. He then scrutinises the aircraft's system pages on our ECAM screens, checking that everything looks in order. These pages will detail the status of every system and highlight any issues.

We also ensure we're monitoring the emergency frequency 121.500 on our secondary radio. This frequency allows ATC to communicate with us should they lose contact on our primary radio, and it's where anyone would transmit if they're in an emergency situation.

In recent years, there's been a strange trend of pilots using 121.500 to make cat noises to each other. Why cat noises as opposed to any other animal? I have no idea. To clarify, I don't condone the behaviour, nor have I participated myself, but I'd be lying if I said I didn't find it amusing each time I hear a "meeeeoooow" on 121.500, followed by a response of meows from other pilots who are clearly also hitting the same level of boredom while cruising the airways.

While on the front of it, it is funny, unfortunately, as with most other parts of the job, there are serious implications to consider here. While the meows are short enough that they wouldn't be 'stepping on' anyone's genuine emergency transmission (& I'm in no doubt that any qualified pilot would never consider interrupting an emergency transmission to get a meow out!), they're probably annoying enough for some pilots to turn off their secondary radio. If they forget to turn it back on, they're putting themselves at risk of not being contactable by ATC if they have issues with their primary radio. If ATC can't reach you on your primary or secondary radio, or via other aircraft around you, their next step would be to scramble fighter jets who will be on your wingtips in minutes, causing a real scare for the passengers and an even bigger one for your company's accountants when they get the bill for the unnecessary interception.

As such, the authorities have recently come down hard on pilots who fulfil their desire to make cat noises on the emergency frequency. ATC now record which aircraft the noises come from and inform the airline of their employees' behaviour. I've heard various stories of disciplinaries and even dismissals happening at other airlines due to this.

As soon as I'm finished confirming that our expected fuel burn and timings from the flight plan match what our aircraft is telling us, I use my MCDU to get some updated weather reports for the airports around us, along with our destination and alternate airports. It's essential for us to have constant situational awareness of what's going on at airfields around us, and always have a plan in our mind of where we'd divert into at any given time should it become necessary.

The printer kicks into life and spews out a long sheet of paper with all the weather reports on it. A quick scan of the text and nothing's jumping out at me. It looks like there's a relatively strong crosswind in Nantes, a city in north-west France that's just off our nose, but it's not enough to cause us any concern unless we had failure that gave us real controllability issues on landing. There's barely any wind down in Bordeaux, an airport further down the west coast, so in my head, I'm already building a rough picture of where I may want to divert, depending on the reason for the diversion.

I send a message to our company through the MCDU, confirming the number of special assistance passengers we have onboard. They'll forward this to our handling agent in Alicante so they can have the appropriate equipment ready for our arrival.

If our flight had been delayed pushing back from the gate, at this point I'd also have to account for every minute of the delay and send the specific reasons to the company in a message. As our delay today was caused after we pushed back, our flight still went down as an on-time departure, so I don't need to send any delay message to the company.

Our arrival time on the box is still showing ten minutes later than planned, although our aircraft is cruising right now at a speed of Mach 0.76, which equates to .76 of the speed of sound. Ben selects the speed knob and turns it to .78. As he does, we feel the engines spool up slightly as the aircraft increases to the new airspeed. Although this increase in speed is minor, we have nearly two hours in the cruise so it can save us a good amount of time over the journey. I look down again at the MCDU's predicted arrival time, and it's now showing just five minutes behind schedule. The estimated fuel we'll be landing with is showing roughly the same as before, so it feels like a good balance of a very slight increase in fuel burn vs time saved.

"Hats off?" I suggest to Ben. This is pilot talk for 'shall we take our headsets off?'. Some pilots insist on wearing their headsets for the duration of the flight. I'm unsure whether this is because they feel they invested so much into an expensive noise cancelling headset so they simply need to make the most of it, or because the ambient noise is genuinely too much for them, but having a chunky old headset on your head for hours on end is never comfortable. Airbus knows this, so they designed the aircraft so that we could take the headsets off during the cruise phase. We have loudspeakers in front of us that amplify ATC's chatter, along with a handheld microphone next to us that enables us to transmit to ATC without having to put our headsets back on each time.

Thankfully Ben's in the same boat as me (or so he says anyway) and gives my suggestion a nod of approval. We both take our headsets off and stow them behind us. The background noise of the flight deck at FL380 becomes instantly apparent.

At the pointy end, we're at the front of this lump of metal forcing its way through the air at over 500mph now. All that's separating us from essentially a 500mph wind, is some glass and a very thin layer of aluminium. This wind, along with the constant pressurised air being pumped through our flight deck via various vents, is now creating some serious background noise. In order to hear ATC over this noise, we have to turn the loudspeakers up loud enough that their voices can be clearly heard, so it does become a rather loud environment.

Pilots have done studies into the damage that this ambient noise level can cause to our hearing and after reading lots of them, I'm in absolutely no doubt that a lifetime of being exposed to this level of noise every day, all day, is damaging to our hearing. As such, I tend to have the ATC chatter on the lowest volume I possibly can while still being able to hear it.

I recline my seat another notch just as the door buzzer goes. I turn to look at the video screen which shows a live feed from the camera in the front galley. I can see John standing outside the locked cockpit door. Just as importantly, I can see two boxes of what I'm almost certain is breakfast in his hands. I check to see that Joel is guarding John, standing behind him and facing the passengers, ensuring nobody's going to try and charge into the flight deck as soon as I open the door, then I reach down and move a small switch by my right hand to 'UNLOCK'. We hear the three bolts slide open on the door, allowing John access to the flight deck.

With his hands full, John pushes the door open with his shoulder and, after entering the flight deck, kicks it shut behind him with his leg. The nutritional value of the food we are served is highly questionable (although porridge is usually a safe enough bet). However, when you've been up since 3:45 a.m., any food smells like good food!

In my airline, the catering company loads staff-specific meals that are different to those offered to passengers. All hot meals come in small plastic containers, similar to what economy passengers on a long haul flight could expect. The breakfast options consist of a few hot choices, usually a very small portion of scrambled eggs, along with some hash browns, sausage, bacon, or something similar. If that doesn't do it for you, there's the option of a small pot of porridge or a mini box of cereal with milk. The breakfasts are glamorously served in cardboard boxes, accompanied by a yoghurt and often a bread roll with some butter. You know you've got a great cabin crew manager when they pop the bread roll in the oven for you so it comes in nice and warm. Unfortunately, this only happens about 10% of the time, although today seems to be our lucky day.

As John hands us our breakfast, along with some warm bread rolls, he makes awestruck noises while looking at the view out the front windows, asking questions about where we are and which cities are around us. I point to the left and explain that Paris is on the horizon, before looking at the stunning view over the Brest peninsula to our right. It comes as a nice reminder for me to not take these views for granted. When we do this every day, it's so easy for us to do so, and to be completely honest, stop appreciating the unique office view we're fortunate to have.

John leaves us so he can continue with their cabin service, and Ben and I enjoy our breakfasts while continuing to chat about Formula One, intermittently interrupted by ATC switching us over to other frequencies as we progress down through French airspace.

Now, although the cruise makes up the longest part of this flight, it takes up the shortest space in this book. Quite simply, that's because we really don't have too much to do during this time and I'm sure you haven't bought this book because you want to read 50 pages filled with mine & Ben's conversations during the cruise (although this book could be a saga?).

We're contacted once every ten minutes or so by ATC while cruising over Europe. It will either be an instruction to change frequency, or to change our heading, speed, or height. In between these calls, the chatter on the radio is often relatively constant, with ATC issuing instructions and receiving readbacks from the various other aircraft also in their airspace. I have to continually be tuned into this, even when relaxing in the cruise or having a conversation with Ben. This skill can be a challenge to learn; being able to hold a conversation with someone while your ears are also listening to constant chatter in the background, and being able to pick up when that chatter is suddenly meant for you. There are times when the cabin crew are in the flight deck for a chat and you'll be having a three-way conversation with them and the other pilot, while remaining tuned into the ATC chatter in the background.

In addition to radio communications, every hour, I do a fuel check, which compares our flight plan fuel to the fuel we have left onboard. This should highlight if we have any fuel leaks. In between fuel checks I'm ensuring we have the most up-to-date weather forecasts for enroute, destination and alternate airports.

As PF, Ben is also responsible for eavesdropping on the ATC chatter, and actioning anything ATC asks us to do if it involves changing the aircraft's trajectory. He's responsible for ensuring the aircraft's autopilot is doing a good job of flying the aircraft, and I'm monitoring this too.

The reality is, though, that apart from the above, we really don't have much to do in the cruise. Some people pass the time with conversation. Other people prefer to do their own thing. Getting through what can sometimes be up to ten hours of cruise time on longer return flights just with conversation, all with someone you've never met before and will likely never meet again, is sometimes quite a stretch.

There aren't really any hard and fast rules on what 'doing your own thing' can consist of, but it's generally understood that it's something that won't pull your attention away from being able to monitor the aircraft and the ATC communications, or lead you to lose situational awareness. It's usually down to the captain what they're happy with and what they deem sensible.

Today, Ben's already informed me he's got his simulator exams starting tomorrow and wants to do more prep for it, so after I've filled him in with everything that was thrown at me over the previous few days in mine to give him an idea of what he can expect, he begins his various bits of revision, which consists of reviewing the company manuals and emergency procedures, while also practicing making landing distance calculations with various failures.

While he does so, I use the quiet time to catch up on my growing list of phone messages and emails that I haven't had a chance to respond to for over a day now. We don't get phone signal or WIFI on board, but I can tee all my messages up to send when I land.

As I've just completed my simulator exams and am also up to date with our yearly 50 question technical exam we have to complete (always reserved to do on a long & dull flight), I don't feel at all guilty pulling the newspaper out of my bag once I'm done on my phone. Told you it would come in handy!

Toilet Break

My reading gets interrupted by a loud buzzer sound after around 30 minutes. I look down to see the 'interphone' light flashing again. The cabin crew are obliged to call us over the interphone regularly. We like to think it's out of the kindness of their heart, but we know it's actually to check whether we're still alive or not.

I hand responsibility for the radios over to Ben, and put my headset on so I can chat to the crew without interfering with any of Ben's communications with ATC.

I press a few buttons to enable me to talk to John, who's on the other end of the cabin interphone. During this time, I still have ATC on quietly in the background of our conversation to monitor it, so I'm still listening to multiple people at once.

It's a quick check-in from John as they're still in the middle of the service. Although he's asking if we'd like anything, I can tell by the tone of his voice that he'd rather we say no, and request anything we do want once they've finished their busy service. I have a bladder the size of a peanut (being an airline pilot was potentially a bad profession choice) so I already could do with a bathroom break. I know what a pain it is for the cabin crew to have to stop their service to allow this to happen, so I ask John to come and let me out once they've finished the passenger service, letting him know there's no rush.

After a little more reading, frequency changes, small talk and daydreaming out the window as we cruise past Bordeaux, the interphone buzzer goes again. John's team have now finished the service and are ready for the bathroom break procedure.

Frustratingly, long gone are the days where we could go to the bathroom at our leisure. This is something my counterparts in the long-haul airlines, who have a toilet in the flight deck compartment, can enjoy, however, on narrow body airliners where we have to enter the passenger cabin to access the toilet, we have strict procedures we have to adhere to before I can take a leak.

Since the Twin Towers attacks in 2001, where multiple aircraft were hijacked, cockpit doors on airliners have remained closed at all times while the engines are running. The only exception to this is when cabin crew need to come in, or one of the flight deck needs a physiological break.

If there were a terrorist on board whose intention was to breach the flight deck, their best chance is when one of the above is happening. Therefore, we now require a 'guard' outside the door, each time the door's going to be opened.

These procedures were taken to a whole new level after the Germanwings incident in 2015, whereby the first officer of Germanwings 9525, who'd been suffering from depression, deliberately locked the captain out of the flight deck when he exited for a toilet break. The first officer then purposely put the aircraft into a fatal descent and flew the A320 aircraft and its occupants into the side of a mountain.

In the immediate aftermath of the disaster, most airlines deemed it unsafe to leave any pilot alone in the flight deck. Our procedures changed overnight, stipulating that there must always be two people in the flight deck. This meant that if one pilot wanted to use the bathroom, not only did a cabin crew member have to guard the cockpit door, but another cabin crew member had to enter the flight deck and remain in there until the pilot returned.

The cabin crew member in the flight deck was tasked with monitoring the lone pilot, and checking that essentially, he or she wasn't trying to commit suicide and mass murder simultaneously. SOPs dictated that the cabin crew must stand behind the pilot, who was to be secured in their seat with all five points of the five-point harness. This would enable the cabin crew to reach back and open the cockpit door manually at the first sign of trouble.

While I can see the logic behind the enhanced procedure, and maybe it brought some relief to passengers onboard to see there were always two people in the cockpit, in my opinion it was a colossal overreaction by the airline industry and one that had multiple flaws.

For starters, there's the metal fire axe located at the back of the flight deck, now within arm's reach of the cabin crew member. The cabin crew member is standing directly behind a pilot who's fully strapped to their seat, unable to move without releasing all their belts. Although both cabin crew and pilots go through rigorous safety checks before being given an airside pass and being allowed to work for an airline, if you're a terrorist organisation or even a solo operator looking to bring an aircraft down in this modern age, are you more likely to do so by going through years of pilot school at great expense, or going through a six week cabin crew training course, before being able to stand in a locked cockpit with access to a metal axe, and one helpless pilot in front of you?

Personally, I never felt comfortable sitting with a cabin crew member I'd never met before, standing directly behind me. I felt safer leaving a pilot who'd invested a substantial amount of time and money into their career, alone in the flight deck, than I did walking out and leaving them rendered essentially helpless should the cabin crew behind them wish to do anything untoward. Not to mention how patronising it felt. How would you feel if the boss of your office job that you've shown loyalty and commitment to over the past ten years, started sending people you'd never met before to sit next to you at your desk to check you aren't trying to strap a bomb to it and blow everyone in the building up?

As well as feeling like we were being babysat and not entrusted not to try and kill everyone onboard that day, the new procedure put even more pressure on pilots to avoid coming out of the flight deck for breaks, as the cabin crew service would now grind to a total halt when we did. It also put more pressure on us to reduce the time spent outside the flight deck during a break to an absolute minimum, as the service was stopped from the moment we left the flight deck to the moment we go back in. Our cabin crew operate on commission, so the more time they're in the cabin selling, the more money they're earning. Their basic wages are so poor that understandably, they're in a hurry to get their cabin crew member back out the flight deck to allow the crew to carry on the service, therefore making more sales.

This unfortunately meant that for pilots, the only real chance to stand up straight and stretch our legs during a flight had now all but disappeared. In the A320, anyone over 6ft can't stand up straight in the flight deck. Standing in the cabin during a toilet break was our only chance to do this for what could be a few hours, as well as giving us an opportunity to have a chat with the crew & build some rapport. After this procedure was introduced, however, all they wanted to do was hurry us back into the flight deck.

It was never the most relaxing experience going into a toilet, knowing that the majority of passengers in the front few rows have seen you go in and are most likely eagerly awaiting you coming back out. On top of this, we now knew we were also under the scrutiny of the cabin crew, who stood outside the door waiting for us to come out.

The final thing the procedure took away from us was the only opportunity to be totally alone all day. When one pilot went to the toilet, it was also often the only time that the other pilot would get any time at all by themselves. We don't get lunchbreaks where you can take yourself off for a quiet wander away from your work colleagues. Nor do we have a quiet corner of the office where we can go and take a breather. From the moment we get on board to the moment we leave, we are constantly 'on' and in the presence of someone directly next to us.

Thankfully, after two years, the airline scrapped the new procedure and reverted to just needing a door guard. However, it still feels uncomfortable to have to make a phone call whenever you need to urinate, followed by lots of watchful gazes as you head into the bathroom.

As I hand the radios over to Ben once again, I jump out of my seat, taking one last look at our estimated landing time, and our exact position on the map as I do so. These hold the answers to the two most common questions I get from passengers when I come out to the toilet, along with "Well if you're out here, who's flying the plane?". It's slightly embarrassing being unable to answer the first two. I often have my own fun answering the third.

I check through the eyehole in our cockpit door that I can see John guarding for my exit before opening it. As I walk out, John lets me know he's locked the toilet door for me, another small touch that us pilots really appreciate. More often than not, there's a queue of passengers at the front of the aircraft waiting for the toilet. A cabin crew member who's on the ball and wants to really help the flight deck out, will lock the toilet door from the outside for us before we come out, and direct the waiting passengers to the rear toilet so we don't have to stand cramped in the middle of a group of passengers waiting our turn for the toilet.

After using the facilities, I use this opportunity to have a quick catchup in the front galley with John and Joel. I want to try to build some rapport while also giving my legs a stretch. I'm acutely aware though that they haven't had a chance to eat breakfast yet and can't do until I'm back in the flight deck, so I keep the chat relatively brief before heading back into our locked box, once again guarded by John. Ben clearly has a bladder of steel, and he refuses the opportunity to use the restroom. Either that or he doesn't trust me alone in the flight deck by myself!

Descent Preparation

About 90 minutes into the flight, as the rugged peaks of the Pyrenees stretch out beneath us in the golden glow of the summer sun, we're handed over to Spanish ATC. We're now around 20 minutes from the start of our descent. It's our cue to shift gears, sharpen our focus and begin preparations for our approach.

Ben will be PF all the way down to the ground (some airlines swap PF/PM roles just before landing), so he starts to input various bits of data into his MCDU. Our flight plan tells us to expect the VLC3L arrival onto runway 10 in Alicante today, but this plan was written a few hours ago so things may have changed. I request the latest ATIS weather report digitally, which confirms that Alicante are indeed still using runway 10 for landing.

Ben and I both bring up the charts for the VLC3L arrival and crosscheck that the information in the aircraft's computer system matches that on the chart. We have an independent look at other charts to build up our situational awareness for what we can expect on the approach. One of these is called a Company Crew Information (CCI) chart, which is created by our company to alert us to the main threats when operating in or out of each specific airfield. It gives us all the essential information we need and shows us any hotspots where incidents usually take place.

We then look at terrain charts to ensure we're aware of the topography of the area before we descend our jet down towards it. Finally, we review the airport ground charts so we're familiar with what things will look like once we've landed. I add all the relevant charts to the digital clipboard on my iPad for quick access. Ben inputs the approach minima from the chart for the ILS approach, but given the weather is spectacularly clear today, it's not a figure we'll be worried about.

The 'minima' is the height at which we must be able to see the runway visually out of the window in order to continue the approach. Our landing guidance instruments may become inaccurate beyond this point on the approach, so we need visual references. Each approach type will have a different minima depending on the accuracy of the approach equipment in use. If you descend to minima and your view of the runway is still obscured by weather, you must conduct a go-around. Our highest minima for the least accurate approach type is around 500ft above the ground. On our most accurate approach type, there is no minima as the aircraft will fly itself all the way down to the runway. These approaches, known as 'autolands' are incredible to see, but are only conducted when the weather conditions are too foggy for the pilots to land themselves.

I commonly get asked "Why don't all planes land themselves all the time if they can?" The short answer is that it's a logistical nightmare for the airport. Due to the high levels of accuracy required from the ground-based landing guidance equipment, larger gaps must be given between arriving and departing aircraft to ensure the radio beams guiding the landing aircraft aren't distorted. This slows down the rate of aircraft flowing into the airfield, which causes large delays.

Another reason is that the current autoland systems also have very restrictive limits on the amount of crosswind they can land in, far less than pilots are capable of landing in manually. I don't think we're too far away from a technological advancement that would allow aircraft to conduct autolands without the requirement for extended gaps in between, as well as an increase in the crosswind limits for the automatic landing system. Watch this space.

With ten minutes to go until the top of the descent, Ben begins his approach briefing the same way he did his departure brief. "Have you had a look through the box?" The structure of the descent brief has also been changed to make the points more relevant and ensure we focus on specific threats as opposed to a monologue from PF.

The main threat we discuss today is the strong possibility of a shortcut on the arrival. The approach programmed into the aircraft takes us 'around the houses' to line us up on final approach. We know from experience, and the fact it's mentioned in the CCI, that ATC down here are likely to offer us a more direct routing on the approach as we get closer to the airport.

If we're offered this short cut in the latter stages of the approach and we hadn't anticipated it, we'll likely either have to refuse it, or if we took it there's a high chance that we'd end up very high on the approach profile, potentially unable to shave off the excess height and speed in time to make a safe approach to the runway.

To mitigate this threat, Ben sensibly reduces the altitude that's programmed into the aircraft's system at the waypoint 'Vilna', which is where we can expect to get the shortcut from. Although the chart states we can't go any lower than 7,000ft at Vilna due to terrain clearance, the aircraft is currently planning to have us overhead that waypoint at 9,000ft as it believes we're doing the much longer approach. By re-programming the aircraft to arrive overhead Vilna at 7,000ft rather than 9,000ft, the aircraft will re-calculate the point at which we must start our descent, and we'll end up in a much better position to accept the shortcut if we get offered it.

Ben briefs me on the 'how to' part of the approach, noting that if it looks like we'll get the shortcut, he plans to have the aircraft slowed right down and partially configured with flaps two selected when we cross Vina. Having our flaps partially extended means the aircraft has a lot of drag, so Ben can dive us down after passing the 7,000ft altitude constraint without a huge increase in our speed, mitigating the chance of us ending up high and fast on the shortened final approach.

He then briefs me on the rest of the approach, where he plans to extend the landing gear, deploy the rest of the flaps, where he'll take the autopilot out, and which taxi routing we're expecting once on the ground. Some companies have very strict rules regarding use of the autopilot, with a few well-known airlines specifying that their pilots cannot manually fly the aircraft above 500ft, so the autopilot must be engaged immediately after take-off and only disengaged again a few moments before touching down.

Our company rules stipulate that we must use 'the highest level of automation appropriate at all times'. I like the way it's worded, as it gives us some wiggle room and autonomy over how we operate the aircraft. At the end of the day, we're highly trained professionals and we got into this job because we enjoy flying planes. Sitting there pushing buttons and watching the autopilot do its thing is cool to see, but it's not real flying.

Where appropriate, of course, I like to 'hand fly' the aircraft for the approach, and openly encourage my first officers to do the same should they wish to. Hand flying consists of disconnecting various parts of the automatics (autopilot and/or auto thrust). We can then take it a step further and do what's known as 'raw data' approaches where we also remove the crosshairs known as flight directors from our PFD. These crosshairs move to where the aircraft thinks you should be flying during the approach. It's pretty easy to just mindlessly follow the flight directors but it engages your brain in another way when you remove them. It takes us back to actually flying an aeroplane, rather than just following what the aircraft is asking us to do.

In the Airbus, manual control is assumed using one of the two sidesticks (mine in my left hand, Ben's in his right) to control the pitch and roll of the aircraft. We then use the thrust levers to control the power. Flying manually really gets the brain working as you've got to keep a rapid scan across various indications in the cockpit; altitude, speed, thrust setting, rate of descent, and heading, all while working out how many track miles you have to run until landing and constantly adjusting the trajectory of the aircraft appropriately.

Hand flying ramps up the workload in the flight deck and reduces capacity for both pilots, as the PF is working harder than usual, and the PM is monitoring harder than usual. PF's task of selecting the speeds, headings, and altitudes into the FCU when requested by ATC now falls to PM, as PF's hands are occupied with the flight controls.

This means the decision to hand fly must be considered carefully. Each situation is different, and various factors must be considered. I have a few hard and fast rules regarding manual flying: If I feel tired, I don't do it. If we're landing at an unfamiliar airport, I don't do it. If we're entering busy, complex airspace with either lots of other aircraft or lots of terrain around, I don't do it. And finally, I'll always ask the FO how they feel and if they're happy with me doing it, if there's any uncertainty, I won't do it.

I'm aware there are many pilots out there who shy away from hand flying. Even worse in my opinion, there are captains who shy away from letting FO's hand fly when there's no excuse not to. It's something that concerns me slightly as there are a variety of failures that could leave the aircraft in a state where the autopilot and auto thrust are not available to use. Although these failures are uncommon in real life, they do happen. In fact, most airlines will allow aircraft to dispatch without the auto thrust working at all.

As a passenger on an aircraft that's unfortunate enough to suffer a failure of the automatic flight systems, therefore requiring the pilot to hand fly, would you rather have a pilot at the controls who regularly practices manually flying and feels comfortable under such conditions, or one who hasn't hand flown a fully manual approach on the real aircraft (except in the sim) in months or even years? Anyway, rant over, let's get back to business.

To conclude Ben's brief, he selects 'autobrake low' on the automatic brake setting and tells me he plans to use 'reverse idle' for this landing.

We have two reverse thrust settings on the A320, 'reverse idle' and 'maximum reverse'. The first is the least powerful form of reverse, engaged by retarding the thrust levers into their first reverse detent, and essentially just changes the way the idle thrust exits the engine. It still takes some of the load off the wheel brakes, but overall, it contributes in a pretty minor way to our deceleration.

On shorter runways when we need to stop quicker, we'll select 'maximum reverse' by retarding the thrust levers to their most rearward position. This spools the engine up and forces air forwards, having a significant effect on slowing the aircraft down. The reasons we don't use maximum reverse unless we really need to are threefold: It's very loud and causes unnecessary noise pollution, likely annoying anyone who lives near the airport. It also increases wear and tear on the engines, and finally, it increases the likelihood of foreign object ingestion into the engine as we're using a high thrust setting on the ground, which would suck any loose objects in the vicinity straight through the engine. All of these things are bad, so we reserve maximum reverse for when we really need it.

The same applies for the different settings we have for the automatic braking system. For landing, we have the option to pre-set either 'low' or 'medium' on the system. 'Low' will automatically apply the wheel brakes in such a way that a comfortable deceleration starts a few seconds after touchdown. 'Medium' will apply a much stronger braking force, that also engages much sooner.

Low braking puts a slight strain on our shoulder straps, while medium braking puts a very noticeable strain on them. For our passengers who don't have the luxury of shoulder straps and are decelerating at the same rate that we are, they're going to be pushed forwards uncomfortably out of their seats.

As well as taking passenger comfort, another factor to consider when deciding which braking mode to use is brake temperatures. The harder and longer the brakes are applied for, the hotter they'll get. Our brake temperatures regularly rise up to above 300 degrees after landing, sometimes edging towards 500 degrees. Having hot brakes underneath an aircraft is never a good thing.

When they do get hot, the brakes take a fair bit of time to cool down. We have a limiting maximum temperature on how hot the brakes can be for take-off, so having hot brakes can become an issue during short turnarounds. A 'turnaround' is the time from when we park at the gate, to when we pushback for the next flight. They're usually between 30 to 45 minutes.

The brake temperature limitation for take-off is there because if we reject the take-off, the brakes are automatically engaged in their strongest mode: Maximum. If you're a passenger on an aircraft with maximum autobrake applied, you'll know about it!

It's strong enough to send any loose articles (or people) to the front of the aircraft. It massively increases the temperature of the brakes, so if they were already too hot in the first place, you'd likely end up with a brake fire. While we have extinguishers in the engines that we can control from the cockpit to put out engine fires, we don't have any extinguishers for the brakes, so having a brake fire is not a nice situation to be in.

If you have a tight turnaround at an airport with a short runway, in a hot country, the issue with brake temperatures can be a real pain and must be managed well.

The short runway means you'll have to apply the brakes heavily on landing, but they won't cool down quickly enough in time for your next departure. To aid the cooling process, our aircraft are equipped with 'brake fans'. These fans make a high-pitched (and very annoying) whining noise as they circulate air over the hot brakes. You'll almost certainly have heard them at some stage if you're a regular flyer. While they can be very effective in cooler conditions at blowing cold air over the brakes and reducing the cooldown time, in warm destinations with a high ambient air temperature, all they really do is blow warm air over the hot brakes.

Again, it's all a game of thinking ahead, being situationally aware and being smart about things. We always select an autobrake option before we land, but at any point the PF can disengage the autobrakes and take over manually by pushing the top of their foot pedals with their toes. It's sometimes difficult to make this a smooth transition, so again you'll likely have felt this slight jolt as the autobrake disengages and the pilot takes over with manual braking.

In the above scenario with a short runway and a tight turnaround, we'd opt to select full reverse and take over the braking manually as soon as we've felt the autobrake engage. Instead of letting the aircraft slam the anchors on until we come to a stop, we'll try to reduce the pressure on the wheel brakes ourselves and use the entirety of the runway to decelerate in an effort to prevent overheating issues that will delay our next departure.

I have no questions following Ben's brief, so he hands me control of the aircraft as he picks up the PA phone to give our passengers an update on our position, arrival time and the weather in Alicante.

After Ben's done talking, there's just one thing left to do; decide how much fuel we want for the return flight. This is just an initial figure and will be re-assessed once we're on the ground, but making one of the most important decisions here is a nice way to buy ourselves some time on what's going to be a very rushed turnaround in Alicante.

We both scroll through the return flight plan on our iPads, again looking for anything that jumps out at us as reasons we should be taking extra fuel.

Nothing out of the ordinary today, however, it's summer and experience tells me we can expect a minimum of 15 minutes of airborne holding as we approach London. We can likely also expect a delaying slot for our departure, which may mean we use a little more fuel as we sit with the APU burning for longer than usual, to supply air conditioning to our passengers while we wait for the slot.

Our main engines will burn a total of 400kg for every ten minutes that we sit in the airborne hold over London. While our flight plan contingency fuel takes account for a little bit of holding, it doesn't give us enough to cover a 15 minute hold. I increase the return fuel figure to allow for it, adding 600kg of fuel in an effort to keep our contingency fuel intact.

Our APU is a much smaller engine and only burns 120kg per hour, so I increase our total fuel figure by another 100kg to give us nearly an hour's worth of APU usage before leaving Alicante in case we get a slot. Ben seems happy with the figure and doesn't wish to add anymore, so it's a done deal for now.

Descent

The point at which we should commence our descent is depicted on our navigation display screen by a downward arrow (original eh!). Starting the descent here will have us arriving at 7000ft overhead Vilna waypoint if we descend at the speeds already programmed into the aircraft (Mach 0.76, which transitions into 280kts later in the descent, before slowing to 250kts as we pass through FL100 to adhere to the speed limits).

ATC are usually pretty good at giving us descent clearance seconds before we ask for it, but today as we're wanting our descent earlier than they'd maybe expect, I request the clearance from them.

"Cleared to descend to FL100 on the Valencia two lima arrival", is the response. Perfect, we've got a nice long descent clearance. Sometimes ATC give us stepped descents if the airspace is busy, clearing us down just one or two thousand feet at a time. This can be a painful process for both the controller and the pilots as it requires constant radio transmissions throughout the descent.

ATC have also given us the arrival, otherwise known as a STAR (STandard ARrival) that we're expecting. If they'd given us a different arrival, we'd have to very quickly change what's programmed into the aircraft and re-brief it accordingly.

Today, as we're anticipating a different arrival or runway from the one on the flight plan, we use the 'secondary flight plan' function in the MDCU and have the shortcut approach set up there. Instead of having to spend time on the approach re-programming the box, we can simply activate this secondary flight plan at the push of a button when we get given the shortcut, meaning the aircraft will then fly that plan.

You'll hopefully have noticed a theme by now, of thinking ahead of the game and anticipating likely scenarios. It's such an important part of flying as it ensures we reduce the workload as much as possible during the most critical phases of flight, giving us more capacity to manage the safe operation of the aircraft. Things can get busy very quickly in the descent, and the last thing you need is to try to brief an approach while you're already halfway through flying it!

Although the aircraft is extremely clever, it occasionally makes mistakes (although admittedly, probably not as often as we humans do!). As such, although the descent software is very accurate, we still run gross error checks throughout the approach using good old mental maths, to work out whether we're high or low on our optimal descent profile.

To do this, we use the three times table to figure out roughly how many miles we require to descend from our current altitude to ground level at a standard rate of descent. Our aircraft takes around three nautical miles to descend 1,000ft, so by multiplying our current altitude by three and then losing the last three 0's, we get the distance we need for the descent.

For example, if we're at 30,000 ft, we times that by three to get 90,000. Minus the three 0's is 90. We'll need roughly 90nm to descend at a normal rate from that altitude to the ground.

This initial calculation gives us a very rough figure, but we can go a step further and fine-tune it. It takes time for us to slow down from our cruising speed to our approach speed. Time in a moving aircraft means distance. The rule of thumb we use is 1nm per 10kts of speed we want to lose. If we're at 280kts now and our final approach speed is 140kts, we've got to add 14nm onto that 90nm to allow us room to slow the aircraft down.

The wind on the approach also plays a factor; if we've got a strong wind behind us (tailwind), our speed over the ground will be substantially higher than if there was no wind. This means we're being pushed towards the runway at a faster rate and therefore will need to start the descent even sooner than normal to allow for it. A similar rule of thumb applies; add 1nm for every 10kts of tailwind.

Jumping back to the previous example, if we had 20 kts of tailwind on the initial approach, we'd need to add 2nm onto our mental calculations, totalling 106nm. You can hopefully see the importance of factoring in the wind and speed adjustments into these calculations, to ensure the top of descent point is correct.

When you've just started your descent and have 100+ miles to go, that 2nm doesn't make too much difference, but remember the need for that mileage will remain until you're on final approach, so as you get closer in, if you forget to include it into your ongoing calculations, you could end up turning onto finals at 8nm and realising you actually need 10nm due to the tailwind, by which point you may find yourself unrecoverably high and have to discontinue that approach, go-around and try again.

As we get closer to the ground, especially below FL100, we often rely mainly on doing this constant mental arithmetic to check we're on the correct descent path and adjust our rate of descent or speed appropriately.

So, what tools do we have at our disposal to adjust this rate of descent? We've got various different modes that we can use for autopilot. One will follow the programmed vertical descent path, ignoring the speed of the aircraft. Another will reduce the thrust to idle and vary the pitch of the aircraft to maintain a set speed during the descent. We also have the ability to set the rate of decent in feet per minute, during which time the aircraft will add thrust as it sees fit, to maintain the desired speed and rate of descent.

If we need to lose speed or height fast, we have wing spoilers we can deploy, which create drag, spoiling the lift effect of the wing and allowing us to descend more rapidly. We can also extend our landing lights to create yet more drag. They drop out from under the wing and although they aren't anywhere near as effective at creating drag as the other tools at our disposal, sometimes every little helps. Another way of creating drag would be to extend the flaps earlier than usual, however, this often requires us to slow down considerably to be below the quite restrictive flap limiting speed, so flaps aren't something we tend to use when we're still far away from the airport.

Our most effective weapon to put the aircraft into an extremely drag induced state is to drop our landing gear. Nothing on the plane will create drag like extending six large tyres, gear doors, and wheel struts into the airflow of the aircraft. If all is going well, we usually only drop the gear a few minutes before landing, but we always have its early extension in our back pockets should we need it.

As we descend through FL200 overhead Valencia, I take a glance at the beautiful city out of the side window. The glass buildings in the city centre shimmer in the morning sun, with the warm terracotta tones of the residential housing closer to the seafront contrasting with the sparkling blue of the Mediterranean Sea.

I can only enjoy the view for a few seconds before turning my attention back inside, where things are starting to get busier in the flight deck. Our headsets are now on, and our focus is fully on the trajectory of the aircraft, along with building our situational awareness of what's going on around us.

I'm already trying to figure out the callsigns of little TCAS blips in front of us on our navigation display. Frustratingly, our aircraft doesn't show us this data, but if I can figure out which blips belong to which callsigns from listening to ATC instructions and seeing which blips do what, we can get even further ahead of the game. When flying into most airports, you'll usually be part of a stream of arriving aircraft being filtered into landing positions in the queue. This can often happen while you're still 100+ miles away from the airfield. This means that you can learn a lot about what ATC might have in store for you by listening to the instructions they give to the aircraft in front of you.

If they put the aircraft in front into the airborne hold, it's likely you'll go into the hold too. In our scenario today, if they offer the shortcut to the aircraft in front of us, and they accept it, it means we can likely expect it to. If, however, that aircraft refuses the shortcut because they weren't prepared for it, or ATC doesn't offer it to them, there's no chance we'll get the offer as it will put us on a crash course with that aircraft. We'd therefore know we can immediately ease off our rate of descent and be higher than 7,000ft at the waypoint we were expecting the shortcut, meaning we save a little bit of fuel.

Passing through FL150, the aircraft's computer indicates we have 20 minutes until landing, but we know the shortcut could save at least six or seven minutes off that time, so we decide to make the PA "Cabin crew please prepare the cabin for landing" while switching on the seatbelt signs. It takes our cabin crew around ten minutes to prepare the cabin, so in situations like this it's another thing we have to think ahead with. If we'd only secured the cabin after getting the shortcut, the crew may not have time to complete all their duties before we got to 500ft, at which point we'd have to go-around due to the cabin not being secure for landing.

It's something that's caught people out many a time at various airports. It's easy to forget to do when you start getting busy and distracted with the business of flying the aircraft onto an approach. I have my own safety net method to remind myself whether I've done it or not; I don't turn on the ILS indicator on my PFD until I've made the PA to prepare the cabin. This means if we're turning onto finals to line up with the runway and I can't see any indications of the ILS data I'm looking for on my screen, it's likely I've forgotten to make the call and will make a very hurried PA letting them know they have around four minutes to do a job that usually takes ten. I'm sure I won't be their best friend that day, but it would hopefully save a go around. Touch wood, I've never forgotten to secure the cabin, yet.

I digitally send off for a final weather report. This gives us the most up-to-date data that we'll put into the aircraft's computer system so it can calculate the most accurate speed possible for our final approach.

We're cleared down to 7,000ft now, and passing through FL100, the aircraft automatically slows down to 250kts. When we switch our altimeter settings from STD (flight levels) to QNH (the local altimeter setting) it's the trigger for us to commence our approach checklist. This checklist makes us both confirm the QNH we have set out loud, along with referencing it to the source of where we got that QNH from, which, in this case, is the digital ATIS.

This amount of crosschecking on the QNH is relatively new, and it's come about due to a very close call in Paris Charles De Gaulle airport where the crew of an Air Hub A320 with 172 passengers on board almost collided with the ground, while over a mile away from the runway. When I say almost, they missed it by 6ft to be exact. This almost catastrophic incident came about because the controller mistakenly gave the crew the wrong QNH figure. Very scary stuff, and a near miss that's worth reading the online reports for if you're interested in it.

Today, with our QNH double and triple crosschecked, we're nearing the waypoint Vilna. We hear the aircraft in front, now overhead the waypoint, being offered a shortcut onto a 10 mile final. There's a joint cheer in our cockpit when they accept it, as it means we're likely going to get the same offer, meaning all our preparation work hasn't been in vain.

Moments later we're told we can expect the shortcut, so Ben starts reducing the aircrafts speed by turning the speed knob on the FCU. The auto thrust does its thing and reduces the thrust to idle, and we watch as the speed trundles its way back through 220kts, now through 200kts. "Flaps one" calls Ben, indicating he'd like me to extend the first stage of flaps. I reach across and place my hand on the flap lever.

My palm is facing backwards, the other way to when I retracted the flaps after departure. This is to indicate I'm planning to pull the flaps lever backwards rather than push it forwards, I call "speed checked, flaps…one". In the air, moving the flaps lever to the first notch in an A320 doesn't actually deploy any flaps. Instead, it extends just the slats at the front of the wing. Slats are in fact lift augmentation devices, so they don't actually slow the aircraft down like flaps do. It's for this reason that we need to select flaps 2, which will extend the flaps from 0 to 2, if we really want to make the plane nice and draggy.

We're now getting very close to the Vilna waypoint and still have a small way to descend if we want to be there at the altitude and speed that Ben had briefed. Ben reaches across the centre pedestal and pulls the speed brake lever with his left hand, partially deploying the wing spoilers. He does what any good pilot would do in a multi-crew environment and shares his thought process out loud to keep me in the loop. "We're a little bit high and fast so I'm going to deploy the speed brake to have us level by Vilna".

The effect of the spoilers is immediately seen and felt. The speed reduces rapidly while simultaneously increasing our rate of descent. As soon as we reduce through 185kts, which is the maximum speed at which we can deploy flap 2, Ben calls for that stage of flap and I select it. As the flaps begin to deploy, he stows the speed brake lever so that the flaps can now do the hard work of slowing the plane down.

Overhead Vilna, we're cleared to make our own way to a ten mile final visually, keeping our own separation from terrain. This means we're fully responsible for setting the altitudes we drop down to, and as such I get the terrain chart up on my iPad showing the lowest altitudes we can safely be at each stage of this descent. Ben and I initially agree that we can descend down to 5,500ft in the section of airspace we're in, so Ben dials this into the FCU and pulls the knob, calling the change in autopilot mode as he does, which is checked by me. He also pulls the aircraft's heading knob, so the heading is now being manipulated by the number he dials into that window, as opposed to the aircraft following the lateral navigation path of the active flight plan. He then asks me to activate the secondary flight plan, and with the click of a button on my MDCU, our navigation display now looks far more sensible as it displays the shortened version of our arrival meaning the distance to go calculated by the aircraft is far more accurate.

A few seconds later, we agree that Ben can set the platform altitude of 3,300ft into the FCU. It's the lowest altitude we'll descend down to until we've picked up the vertical glideslope indicator for the ILS. As we continue this descent, Ben starts to finesse the rate of descent using the knob on the FCU. Thanks to his preparation earlier, we're now on a really nice vertical profile for the approach, so we don't need to descend so rapidly anymore.

Around a minute later, after more finessing from Ben, we're about to cross the runway's extended centreline, still 11 miles away from the airfield. Ben's already engaged the approach mode, so as we intercept the lateral localiser signal from the runway, the aircraft starts turning to line itself up with runway 10. During the turn, our cabin intercom buzzer goes, and before I've had a chance to answer it, ATC instruct me to transfer the frequency onto the tower frequency.

Time to prioritise again. I don't think Ben is anticipating dropping the landing gear in the next ten seconds, so while monitoring the aircraft's capture of the localiser, I ignore the cabin crew call for now and respond to the ATC message. I was one step ahead and made sure I had the tower frequency dialled into our standby frequency, so it's a quick readback before I flick to the tower frequency and check in with them.

I receive the exact short and sharp response I expect, "Hola, continue approach runway 10, one ahead to land, wind 140 degrees 12 knots". I read back the only part of that transmission we need to "Continue approach runway 10". I can see the vertical glideslope indicator now about an inch above where it needs to be on our PFD for us to capture it, and to start descending on the final descent profile, which equates to roughly another 20 seconds. It feels like a good opportunity to answer that cabin call, so I hand Ben the radios and select the interphone.

At the other end of the interphone is John, who is calling to let us know the cabin is secured for landing. I thank him, and end the call, reaching forward and flicking the plastic flipper from 'secured for take-off' to 'secured for landing'. This is probably one of the most old school pieces of equipment in the flightdeck, but hey, it works!

I take the radios back from Ben, just as he's announcing "glideslope star", indicating that the Airbus has captured the vertical glideslope beam from the runway, as it pitches the nose down to begin our final approach.

Things are looking good. The aircraft's speed is stable at 180kts, we're configured with flaps 2 and fully established on the ILS with just under 10 miles to run until touchdown.

Approach

Despite the fact we're in one of the most critical phases of flight and descending towards the ground at around 800 feet per minute, there's silence in the flight deck, and hopefully an air of calm exuding from myself & Ben. We're both in our respective zones, monitoring the
100

autopilot as it flies the aircraft down the approach, and counting down to the six mile mark where Ben briefed that he'd ask me to drop the landing gear.

I use the gap between tasks to pre-tune the ground frequency into our radios, so I don't have to be looking down and fiddling with the tuner while also vacating the runway at speed.

I keep an eye out the window on the aircraft in front, a Ryanair 737, as they touchdown in the distance. I note to Ben that it looks like they've missed the first taxiway to vacate the runway. Ben understands what I'm implying without me having to spell it out; he asks me to drop the gear earlier than briefed in order to slow our aircraft down sooner. The preceding aircraft will now have to roll further down the runway until they can get off at the next taxiway, and we won't be allowed to touchdown until they've completely vacated. By slowing down earlier, we're reducing our chances of having to do a go-around due to the runway still being occupied.

I lean forwards and pull the gear lever down, as Ben simultaneously pushes the speed knob on the FCU. This brings the thrust back to idle as the aircraft slows itself down to our final approach speed. My right hand automatically moves around the flight deck to complete the flow that dropping the gear starts; pulling the ground spoiler lever to arm them so that they'll deploy when we touch down, then my hand moves up to the landing lights to turn all of them on. There's lots of thuds, bangs, and hydraulic noises as the gear drops down and locks into place. No sooner than it does, I'm selecting flap 3 under Ben's request to help our speed decay even faster.

We're now in the final landing configuration. Our aircraft can be configured with a further stage of flaps (flaps full), however, it causes lots more drag, which can sometimes be unnecessary. In the name of fuel saving, we're encouraged to complete flap 3 landings where possible and for the majority of airports, there isn't much difference in the flight deck whether we do flap 3 or full.

The next event happens just a few moments later, as we pass through 1,000ft above the airport. The aircraft calls "1,000", at which point we need to have met a certain set of criteria to continue the approach. We must be in the landing configuration, and the speed must be within certain parameters. If these aren't met, we have to conduct a go around.

Ben acknowledges the 1,000ft callout and confirms we meet the criteria to continue. He then requests the landing checklist which ensures the aircraft is fully prepared for touchdown.

The next call's going to be at 500ft, by which point there are even stricter criteria that must be met. We're on track to meet these, so Ben presses his big red button on his sidestick which disconnects the autopilot, accompanied by a loud triple chime from the flight deck speakers. In his brief, he sensibly noted he didn't desire to do much manual flying due to the very early start this morning. While he could technically keep the autopilot engaged all the way down to a few moments before landing, he wants to get a feel of the aircraft in the current conditions ahead of the landing, hence the decision to take it out just before 500ft.

I see the Ryanair now vacating the runway to the left, which is a welcome sight. I can already tell, however, that it may pose another problem. As they've travelled too far down the runway, when they get on the taxiway they're going to taxi towards us to get to the terminal. If Ben aces the landing and puts the plane down in the right spot, which I'm confident he will, we'll be vacating at the first rapid exit taxiway, likely leaving us hurtling towards that aircraft head on and trying to share the same bit of taxiway at the same time. I make a mental note to keep an eye on their taxi progress and bring my focus back to the task at hand; monitoring Ben landing the thing.

Ben's now fully in his zone. His focus is mostly on his instruments, with the occasional glance outside, making small corrections on his sidestick.

Flying the Airbus takes a bit of getting used to as it's such a clever piece of equipment. Any input to the sidestick doesn't actually move the flight control surfaces directly. Instead, it sends an electronic signal to one of seven flight control computers, which then sends another signal to the servos on the applicable flight control. This is the meaning of 'fly by wire'. This also means there's no direct feedback to the sidestick, so when the aircraft moves around during an approach, it's impossible to 'feel' what's happening through your flight control stick as you could in a more conventional aircraft, because the stick's not moving.

What's even more challenging, is that a captain can't feel what a first officer is doing. I have a sidestick on my side, which my hand is firmly planted on during the approach, however, the stick doesn't move. The first officer's stick is on the far side of the flight deck and is almost concealed from my view, so it's hard for me to judge the inputs that are being made by the first officer.

This control set up played a large part in the infamous crash of Air France 447, during which one of the pilots mistakenly held the sidestick fully back while the aircraft was in a stall, when the aircraft actually needed the complete opposite input to correct the situation.

Unfortunately, the aircraft had also suffered a failure that prevented it from overriding this incorrect pilot input, and automatically pitching the nose of the aircraft down to get itself out of the stall situation. The other pilot was unaware of the input being made by the first officer. Although both pilots were startled and confused, one pilot tried the correct action and pushed his sidestick forwards in an attempt to escape the stall. Unfortunately, he didn't use the red takeover button on his sidestick when doing so. If he had, it may have saved 228 lives.

If both sidesticks are moved at the same time, the Airbus takes the sum of the inputs of the two sidesticks. In this scenario, by pushing the stick forwards, that pilot was simply counteracting the other pilot's full back stick deflection. The input to the flight control surface was nil, as the two inputs cancelled each other out, therefore the aircraft remained in a stall, plummeting out of the sky at over 10,000 feet per minute, or 200kmph.

In addition to disconnecting the autopilot, the red button on the sidestick can be used to give each stick priority over the other. If one pilot pushes and holds the button, the aircraft will ignore any inputs made from the other stick. If, however, the other pilot then pushes their red button, that stick is then the one that's listened to, temporarily locking the other stick out. If one pilot holds their button for over 45 seconds, it locks the other stick out permanently, which can be a lifesaving feature in the case of a sidestick fault.

This all sounds potentially dangerous and complicated, so you may be asking why do they make planes fly-by-wire? Although it has some limitations, overall, it's far safer than conventional aircraft in which the cockpit controls are connected to the flight control surfaces directly via pulleys and cables.

For a start, these pulleys and cables can be prone to wear & tear, which computers aren't. Also, in a fly-by-wire system, the computer decides whether the control input you're trying to make is safe. If it's not, it'll disregard your input. If all systems are working correctly, the flight control computers can also take over if they decide that the aircraft is in serious trouble, such as about to stall. The computer has the ability to manipulate the flight controls in such a way to prevent the aircraft from ending up in this state, with the ability to override the pilot input if it's only going to make the situation worse.

Airbus were one of the first companies to introduce fly-by-wire into a mass market airliner back in the 1980s, met by much scepticism. This wasn't helped when one of the first flights to show off the new aircraft ended up crashing into a forest – Air France 296Q. Although the software and computer systems were arguably not the cause of that crash in the first place, since then, the software has come a long way and now all new airliners from manufacturers across the board are fly-by-wire.

Due to our aircraft having this technology onboard, it can do some very clever things such as correct itself when it's being knocked around by wind on the approach. If one of the wings gets lifted due to a gust of wind, the aircraft will correct itself and bring itself back to wings level, even without the autopilot engaged. Very few smaller training aircraft have this feature, so it can be instinctive for new pilots on this machine to correct the initial deviation caused by the wind, at the same time that the plane is. This can lead to 'over controlling', and you'll end up waggling the wings all the way down the approach. The Airbus requires a delicate touch on the sidestick (apart from when landing in a storm), it can quite literally be flown with just your finger and thumb on the stick.

Touchdown

Ben's doing a grand job of flying the aircraft smoothly down the approach path and not overcorrecting. The aircraft announces "500" as we pass through the check height, which is a cue for me to ensure all of the criteria are met. Before calling "stable", I need to check that our airspeed, rate of descent, bank angle, cabin status, landing configuration, vertical and lateral path are all as they need to be. I've been monitoring all these parameters all the way down the approach anyway, ready to make specific callouts should any of them surpass certain limits. Above 500ft, if these parameters aren't met, Ben has a chance to correct them. As we pass through 500ft, however, they all must be met. If they aren't, I have to call "not stable", closely followed by "go-around".

Thankfully today they are, so Ben responds "checked" to my call of "stable". As we transition through the final few hundred feet of the approach, Ben shifts his attention almost solely outside the aircraft, relying less on his instruments and more on the visual picture of the runway to bring us down towards the correct touchdown point. My job as PM becomes even more crucial here, as I'll need to keep an eye on our instrument parameters to ensure we're not straying beyond any limits.

The 500ft call was also my personal cue to give everything inside the flight deck a final once over visually. It's not SOP, but I think it's good airmanship and a chance to catch anything we may have missed. Although the aircraft will generally tell us if any of the major bits aren't done yet, and the checklist will likely pick anything else up, I still like to do my own checks.

I start up top, running my eyes across the overhead panel, looking for anything out of place or any buttons illuminated that shouldn't be. My visual scan then comes down to the FCU, then down to the central pedestal. I take a look across to Ben's screens, then mine. A final check of the approach speed on my MCDU compared to that on the PFD, along with the automatic brake setting selected by Ben, and I'm satisfied we're in good shape to land and stop.

Finally, I type our callsign into my MCDU. So far, it's been displayed at the top of my MCDU for the entirety of the flight, but as soon as we touchdown this data will be automatically wiped. As every flight has a different callsign, it's not uncommon to have totally forgotten your callsign that flight when it's no longer written in front of you. By typing it into the MCDU now, I know it'll remain there even when the rest of the data disappears. This small trick prevents an embarrassing moment when I tune into the ground frequency and have to scramble around on my iPad flight plans to find our callsign.

Passing through 200ft now, Ben's gaze remains almost fully outside. The other aircraft has vacated the runway, and ATC gives us our landing clearance.

My thumb rests on the red takeover button on my side. As the captain, it's my responsibility to take over if I feel things are unsafe at any point. Although Ben's done a grand job so far, I've never flown with him before today. While the general calibre of our first officers is great, I don't know Ben's precise ability level, or how he'll perform in the final few seconds of the landing, which is the most critical part of the flight. Due to our proximity to the ground during this phase, there's little time to correct mistakes.

Ben's got his eyes on the runway aiming point, which is indicated by two large painted rectangles on the runway. This is where we'd ideally like the main wheels to touchdown. We see two smaller sets of these white rectangles as we look further down the runway. The final set depicts the end of the 'touchdown zone', the area in which the main wheels *must* touch down. If we haven't touched down by the time we reach the final set of touchdown zone markers, we must conduct a 'balked landing' which consists of me pushing my red button, taking control, and applying full thrust to climb the aircraft into the air for another go. There may not be enough runway for us to stop should we land beyond these markers.

Getting the aircraft arriving at the aiming point accurately can be a challenge itself, but the next challenge comes when you flare the aircraft. This is the process of raising the nose to reduce the rate of descent just before the wheels touch down, preventing the aircraft smashing into the ground at 700fpm. Although our landing gear is technically capable of withstanding this impact, it really wouldn't be a fun ride for the passengers.

Flaring at the right time, and with the correct amount of backstick is a very dynamic manoeuvre and each flare will be slightly different. You must consider the wind, the rate of descent, the airspeed, the aircraft's weight, and how long your touchdown zone is, when deciding how much backstick you want to apply and when.

Starting the flare, however, is not the end of it. You must 'fly' the aircraft onto the ground. This means making continuous minor adjustments on the sidestick in order to get the wheels to touchdown smoothly in the right spot. Once the main wheels are down, you still need to fly the nosewheel onto the ground. Releasing all the back pressure on the sidestick as soon as the rear wheels touch would result in the nosewheel smashing into the tarmac and possibly lead to an extremely uncomfortable bouncing effect. Instead, we have to delicately reduce the pitch of the aircraft using the stick, to gently lower the wheel onto the ground as the aircraft begins decelerating.

It takes a long time to build your capacity to a level where you can absorb all the required information in a few seconds and then apply the appropriate input during the flare, but once you're able to, it's a really satisfying feeling.

Today, we're in standard weather conditions with an average aircraft weight and normal approach speed, so I'm expecting Ben to begin a gentle flare just before 20ft above the ground. We cross the runway threshold, travelling at 140kts, and the plane announces '50', indicating we're 50ft above the runway. Ben now shifts his gaze beyond the runway aiming point and towards the horizon.

Continuing to focus on the aiming point in the flare will almost certainly lead to a very heavy landing. By looking up at the horizon, Ben's able to use his peripheral vision to judge our rate of descent and adjust it appropriately.

I circle my thumb over the red takeover button on my sidestick, as I always do at 50ft, to check it's definitely on it and remind myself of my duty to take control if this flare or landing doesn't go to plan.

A few seconds later, the aircraft announces '40', then '30'. The length of time between these calls gives us a good sense of our rate of descent.

I now raise my gaze away from the instruments and toward the end of the runway so I can also judge the closure rate of the aircraft to the ground, which is rushing up to meet us at a rate of knots.

Ben begins to gently apply backpressure on his sidestick to raise the nose of the aircraft, while simultaneously retarding the thrust levers, reducing the engine power to idle.

Next, we hear '20'. The time between these height callouts now should increase as our rate of descent is reducing. The delay between '20' and '10' however feels too long.

Our rate of descent has reduced too fast as Ben's lifted the nose of the aircraft ever so slightly too quickly and 'floated' the aircraft. The danger now is that we land long, outside the touchdown zone. My thumb still rests on the red takeover button, ready to react if Ben doesn't correct this in the next few seconds. My eyes are now firmly fixed on the final set of touchdown zone markers which we're rapidly approaching. His intuition kicks in, and he reduces the back pressure applied to his sidestick, allowing the nose to drop ever so slightly so we can continue to descend.

Due to the extended time in this flare with no thrust applied to the engines, the aircraft is losing speed fast. This actually helps us by adding a sinking effect, but in turn can lead to a very firm landing if we sink too fast. The next threat is that Ben could try to overcorrect for this sink, lifting the nose too much to try and cushion the firm landing, which can actually lead to the tail of the aircraft hitting the ground.

This is where it would be very handy to know the true ability and capacity of the person next to you! Thankfully, Ben does a textbook job of recovering the early flare. He adds just a slight pitch up before the main wheels make contact with the ground, but not enough to risk striking the tail on the runway.

There's a bump as the main wheels connect with the ground, and Ben immediately moves the thrust levers into the reverse dent. The ground spoilers automatically deploy to kill any remaining lift the wings were giving us. The automatic braking system doesn't kick in until two seconds after we touchdown, so there's a delay until we start to feel the force of the declaration against our shoulder straps, pushing us forward in our seats.

I bring my attention back inside the flight deck to monitor and announce a few items. "Ground spoilers" as I check that our system display shows they've deployed across both wings. "Reverse green" indicating that reverse thrust is engaged. "Decel", confirming that our speed is decreasing, and that a small 'DECEL' light is showing below our autobrake buttons.

As I'm doing this, Ben gently lowers the nosewheel onto the ground, and we feel a small jolt as the stationary wheel touches the tarmac at around 120kts. As our aircraft decelerates through 70 kts, I call the speed out to give some reference to Ben, who's attention is still fully outside.

He's currently in the process of deciding which taxiway exit to take, while applying pressure to the lower half of his rudder pedals to keep the aircraft on the runway centreline.

As we landed a little deep into the touchdown zone due to the slight float, we're now approaching our planned vacating taxiway at a higher speed than briefed. If Ben leaves the low auto brake setting engaged on the wheel brakes, we aren't going to slow down sufficiently to take the first exit and will have to imitate the aircraft that landed in front of us. Ben decides to disengage the system by pushing with his toes, calling "manual brakes" as he does, and applies more brake pressure to increase the rate of deceleration. He's going for it!

The issue I considered earlier in my head looks like it's about to unfold next. The aircraft that missed vacating the runway at the first taxiway is now approaching our rapid exit taxiway from the other direction. We'll be vacating the runway still at a speed of around 45 kts, straight into the path of the Ryanair. Either Ben's going to have to really put the anchors on to stop before that taxiway intersection, or the Ryanair needs to stop where they are and give way to us.

The latter would be the more logical thing to do as we're not only travelling a lot faster than them, but we're also the ones trying to get off an active runway. The last thing we want is to be sat stationary with the rear half of our aircraft still on the active runway at a Spanish airport, where we're unable to see what's potentially hurtling down the runway towards us. Needless to mention, Ryanair are the ones who couldn't put their plane down in the right spot....

At this point, ATC may be unsure which taxiway we're looking to vacate as it's hard for them to judge our level of deceleration, so I give them a nudge. "Vacating charlie four" is all I need to say to get the ball rolling. ATC immediately orders the Ryanair aircraft to stop and give way to us. Hah!

Before their PM has even read the instruction back, I see the taxi light on their nosewheel turn off, which immediately gives me faith that they've received the message. This is a bit of an unwritten rule between pilots; whoever has the right of way keeps their taxi light on, and whoever is giving way turns theirs off.

It's good news for us as not only can Ben keep the speed up as we vacate, but we're also getting to jump in front of the Ryanair for the taxi in, saving us a further minute.

Taxi In

Still slowing through 40kts as we make the 45 degree turn onto the rapid exit taxiway, Ben transitions from using his rudder pedals to steer the aircraft's nosewheel, to his handheld tiller located just behind his sidestick. As he does, I'm instructed to change to the ground frequency. I know from experience it's a short taxi from the runway to the gate here, so as soon as Ben's completed his post landing flow of disarming the ground spoilers and turning off the landing lights, I begin mine, while simultaneously transmitting to ground that we've vacated the runway. My hand moves across to retract the flaps, then turn the weather radar off. Ground ATC welcomes us and gives us the exact taxi routing we were expecting, to gate 33, which is only 100 meters in front of us.

They've dispatched a 'follow me' car, which they always do here for some unbeknown reason. These cars drive in front of the aircraft, leading us to our gate. They're nowhere to be seen at large, complex airports where aircraft routinely get lost, however, you can always trust you'll find one at an airport where it's nearly impossible to get lost.

110

Alicante is one of these airports, as it's essentially a single taxiway past the terminal with all the gates very clearly numbered. Thankfully, I see all the airlines receiving the same level of unnecessary service when I come here, so it's not a sign of the airport's specific distrust of my company's ability to taxi to the correct gate!

After reading back the taxi clearance and gate number, which I also write into my MCDU so we don't forget it, my right hand moves around the flight deck to complete my post-landing flow. Ben makes a polite gesture to the giving way Ryanair pilots as we cross in front of their now stationary aircraft. Large planes are never close enough to see the faces of other pilots in detail, but you can always make out hand signals.

This proved highly amusing when I used to operate from the smaller base and knew who the pilots on the other aircraft around us were by their voice on the radio. I did, however, get caught out one day when making a not-so-polite gesture out the front of our flight deck, towards my friend in another flight deck whose aircraft was taxiing perpendicular to ours. I totally forgot about the 26 passenger windows that were also facing the front of our aircraft….Lesson learnt!

Today, there's no response from the Ryanair pilots. They're likely making another not so polite gesture just below their window that they'd rather our passengers not catch sight of. I can't blame them to be fair. Should've done a better landing!

As I reach up to start our APU prior to parking, I see the yellow follow-me car with flashing lights on it pull in front of us and start directing us to our gate. While my hand's already up on the overhead panel, I switch off our taxi light so as to not blind the car driver in his rear view mirror.

My hand then drops down onto the central pedestal to change the transponder to ground mode, I then reset a few buttons on the FCU before finally checking that the APU is starting correctly. It takes about a minute to spool up, and we'll need it running before we shut our engines down.

As well as needing a warmup period before departure, our engines also need a cool down period of three minutes after landing before we switch them off. I prod some buttons on my MCDU, which tells me the exact second the aircraft touched down. I call out loud the time that we're looking for with the three minutes, to the second, "Forty six, thirty three". To an outsider, it would look like I'm saying random numbers to myself and maybe going a bit crazy, but luckily, Ben's been here long enough to know exactly what that means without the need for any accompanying explanation from myself.

As it's such a short taxi, we're already almost at our gate, but we still have to wait for our APU to start fully. Where possible, we want to avoid coming to a stop at the gate and leaving the engines running for any length of time. Although the red flashing beacon on the aircraft will indicate to the ground crew that the engines are still running, they're used to aircraft switching off their engines as soon as they come to a halt on stand.

There are many horror stories out there that involve ground crew being turned into mincemeat and discharged out the rear of the engine in small pieces, because they approached an engine that was still running.

To reduce our chances of this, we try to hit the three-minute engine cool down period *before* we come to a stop. Ben reacts to my timing call with a further application of brakes, slowing the aircraft down to buy us a little more time. The follow-me car has now reached our stand number and has turned towards it, accelerating away from us, so it won't be blocking our approach. I take one last scan across the flight deck to check I've done everything I need to. It's been a very busy two minutes with lots going on. With all the distractions and interruptions to flows, it's incredibly easy to forget things like retracting the flaps or starting the APU, both of which can lead to lots of embarrassment when you arrive on stand.

If you shut down the engines without an APU running, the aircraft will lose all power to its electrics. In the daytime, this may not even be noticeable to the passengers. At nighttime, however, when the cabin is suddenly plunged into darkness, it's a real red-faced moment for the pilots.

I believe forgetting to start the APU is a rite of passage for any airline pilot. It's a mistake you need to make once, to ensure you never do it again. My red-faced moment did indeed come at night, at the end of an extremely long and tiring day. We'd just had new company guidance introduced which encouraged us not to start the APU in our after landing flows, and instead start it when we're around one minute from the parking gate to save fuel. On this occasion it was a long taxi in, so by the time we were arriving at the taxi gate, I'd totally forgotten I hadn't started the APU as it would've been out of my normal sequence to be starting it now. I didn't do the final cross check of the APU that I've now learnt to do before turning onto stand, and sure enough when I turned the engines off, we were all plunged into darkness, closely followed by a few expletives from myself as I reached up to start the APU, then waited for what felt like the longest minute of my life until it spooled up enough to provide us power again.

Today is looking like it'll be a better day, and just as we're about to turn onto the stand, Ben hands me control of the aircraft. Our company procedures dictate that only the captain can turn the aircraft onto stand and park it, but it's more lenient than some airlines where they don't even let first officers taxi at all.

I assume control verbally, while placing my left hand on the tiller and right hand on the thrust levers. I slow the aircraft down even more, while looking at our brake indicator to check the parking brake will have pressure when I apply it. Next, I look up to check that the stand parking guidance system screen is displaying the correct aircraft type. This system is about to guide us down the stand's centreline and tell me when to stop, so it's imperative that it knows how big our aircraft is.

A quick final look to check that the array of people, objects and vehicles ready to pounce on our aircraft, are all located behind the red lines on the stand, and I turn the nose of the aircraft to the right to line it up with the stand's centreline. I glance down to our clock, which still shows 30 seconds remaining until we can shut the engine down. I let the aircraft edge onto the stand, slower than walking pace, to try and drag this one out.

Our passengers will likely be confused as to why they could crawl towards the terminal faster than we're moving to it, but the ground crew will be aware, they're likely used to pilots trying to do this for the safety reasons mentioned before. As soon as we're aligned on the centreline, still 20 meters to go, Ben makes a PA through his headset microphone "cabin crew disarm doors for arrival". This is their signal to leave their seats and disarm the cabin doors. The doors were 'armed' when we pushed back off the stand in London. If the door is opened when armed, the emergency escape slide automatically deploys. While this is great in an emergency, it's not what you want when parked on stand, so the cabin crew must manually disarm the doors by moving a lever. They have to crosscheck this with each other and finally with us in the flight deck before opening the door.

There have been many incidents across the airline world where doors have been mistakenly left armed and then opened on stand, triggering the emergency slide to deploy, usually causing injuries to ground crew going about their business around the aircraft. Also, if there were an incident this close to stand requiring an evacuation of the aircraft, it may not be a great idea to evacuate via the aircraft's slides as going down them could send the passengers straight into the side of a baggage truck, so they're always disarmed before we come to a stop.

As we creep towards our stopping mark, I'm fully focused on three things: our ground speed, the clock, and the guidance screen in front of me. The screen gives me a countdown in meters, showing how far away I am from the stop mark. It also gives me correction indications left and right to ensure our nose wheel is bang in the middle of the centreline. In the last five meters I slow the aircraft to a snail's pace. Just as the guidance board flashes "STOP", we've had our three minutes exactly. Perfect. I hold my feet on the brake pedals as I reach down and apply the parking brake, checking that the pressure indicator shows it's engaged before releasing my feet.

I take one quick glance up to check the APU is definitely running before switching both the Engine master 1 and Engine master 2 off. As we hear the engines winding down, my hand goes up to the overhead panel in preparation for the next action. My thumb rests itself on the beacon light switch, and my index finger on the seatbelt switch. I look down at the N1 engine fan speeds and as soon as they're both below 10%, I switch the beacon off, indicating to the groundcrew that it's safe to approach. I glance down to our door indication page and check that all the doors are showing as disarmed, before switching off the seatbelt signs. I do this fully in the knowledge that most of our impatient passengers have usually already stood up at this point, much to the dismay of the cabin crew. I've never understood why everyone's so keen to jump up immediately, sometimes before the aircraft even comes to a complete stop, only to then have to wait a further ten minutes before you can actually get off.

Ben's hand now darts around the flight deck, turning our transponder and fuel pumps off. He then turns on the air conditioning in the cabin, which is now supplied by the APU as our engines are no longer supplying pressurised air. I watch as the swarm of people and vehicles descend on the aircraft. Technically what's known as 'the turnaround' has just begun.

The Turnaround

The first few members of ground crew pace towards the front of the aircraft to put chocks in place. These will prevent the aircraft rolling backwards should the park brake fail at any point. The jet bridge kicks into life and the operator starts manoeuvring it towards the aircraft as our interphone buzzer rings. I answer the call while instinctively looking at our door systems page once again. As expected, it's John, phoning for my confirmation that the doors are showing as disarmed on our systems display screen.

As I confirm this with John, I see a member of the ground crew waving for my attention outside. He signals that the chocks are in place. I give him a thumbs up, before ending the call with John, then asking Ben for the parking checklist. As with the previous checklists, it's there for us to confirm we've done everything we need to do and make sure we haven't overlooked anything. The checklist contains items as obvious as 'engines', to which I must look at and respond "off". While these seem patronisingly obvious, they're on there for a reason. I personally know of a crew at another airline who only realised they still had both engines running when they got to the item on the checklist. I imagine their faces went a much darker shade of red than mine did during my APU fiasco.

Before I continue with the tasks I have to do before this flight is officially complete, I stand up and open the cockpit door. Some pilots leave this shut until such times as they actually need to go out into the cabin for something during the turnaround, but I think opening it at the earliest opportunity adds to the feeling of inclusiveness and being a team, which I tried to focus on at the start of the day. It's also very handy for the cabin crew, who know they're now welcome into the flight deck to check out the window on the status of the jet bridge.

A quick glance up at the guidance screen in front now shows '-30', along with our outbound flight number. We have exactly 30 minutes from now, before we're due to be releasing our parking brake and pushing back for our next flight. This is standard stuff for us. During the next 30 minutes, it'll be all hands on deck from every party involved to make this work. The turnarounds are optimised down to the minute, and we have set tasks that have to be completed within the timeframe. When it goes well, it's like a carefully choreographed show with various teams and people working with and around each other. Unfortunately, due to how optimised it is, it's easy for one small thing to bring the whole turnaround to a grinding halt.

Beyond the guidance screen, I can see our next load of passengers lining up inside the gate. We haven't even opened the aircraft door from the inbound flight yet!

As PM, I still have some final tasks to complete to wrap up our first sector, as well as various captain duties, so I swing myself straight back into my seat. I have to input our take-off and landing times, along with taxi times and shutdown fuel from the aircraft's computer into my iPad's flight plan. I then need to check that everything else has been correctly recorded on the flight plan to fulfil regulatory requirements before digitally sending it off to our HQ back in the UK.

Next up, I grab the tech log from behind my seat as I hear the front left hand door of the aircraft open. Ben whips out the fuel chart and asks if I'm still happy with the fuel we agreed on during the flight. We have a very quick brainstorm for reasons to take more, but can't find any legitimate ones, so he puts the card in the window for the fueller to see when he arrives, before jumping up and announcing that he's going to say goodbye to a few passengers from the front of the cabin. We're encouraged to do this at our airline, and it's nice to actually see the passengers we've flown, but quite often we just don't have time.

Before opening the tech log, I enter the next flight number and destination into the MCDU. This enables me to send a request to download the next flight plan route directly to the aircraft. It saves me having to manually build the route and typing in every single waypoint and airway, which can be very time-consuming. The download usually takes a few minutes, so I always try to get the ball rolling as early as possible. It may sound crazy that in the cockpit, we're already preparing the aircraft for the next flight while we still have the previous load of passengers on, but with such short turnaround times, we've become accustomed to it.

Back to the tech log, and I have to scribble in some more information regarding the flight details, timings, shutdown fuel, and whether we experienced any defect or failures during the flight. If we did, I'll need to write them into this book and then call our engineering department back in the UK before we dispatch the aircraft again. Some minor defects I can legally sign off myself, which will allow us to fly the aircraft home. More serious ones will need to be checked over by a qualified engineer before we depart. Thankfully, we have engineering coverage in almost every destination we fly to, which is very good for peace of mind.

While I'm still finishing off my tech log entries, we hear a loud thump on the right-hand side of the fuselage. Ben comes back into the flight deck to look out of his side window, noting the ground crew signalling that they've connected the external ground power. I reach up to select the ground power on the overhead panel, but don't turn the APU off just yet as there are still quite a few passengers on the aircraft who'll appreciate the continued air conditioning.

Ben now grabs his high visibility vest and declares he'll go and begin his walkaround. He slots himself into the string of disembarking passengers before disappearing through the jet bridge side door to do a repeat of the walkaround I did in the UK.

He's got the better end of the deal here. He's the only one out of the whole crew who'll actually get off the aircraft and properly stretch his legs in the sun. I then glance down as my MCDU flashes up with a message to tell me my flight plan's been successfully downloaded, and I let out a sigh of relief as it's just saved me around five minutes of work.

Now that Ben's PM and I'm PF, it's Ben's responsibility to get the weather, along with the various other bits of information that I had to fetch back in London. On tight turnarounds, however, we're a team, and we help each other out where we can. Ben's getting ahead of the game by getting the walkaround done nice and early, so I start the process of requesting the latest weather in my MCDU, before jumping back to my flight plan page to start inputting the various bits of data that will be specific to our expected departure and arrival today.

The work that needs doing in the MCDU to set the aircraft up takes around 20 minutes when you first start out in the airlines. Over time, pilots tend to be able to slash this time almost in half. There's a slight delay from when you click a button on the MCDU, to when the MCDU actions your input. After a few years of setting the aircraft up for departure, most pilots are able to press buttons continuously at lightning speed, without actually waiting for the MCDU to catch up before the next button is pressed. This would look totally overwhelming to someone just starting out, it's also not a suggested method by our airline, or any airline, but when you've pushed the same buttons in the same order for almost a decade, it tends to become second nature. I'm very often selecting buttons that aren't correlated with anything on the current MCDU page, but I've already selected another page that has yet to change on the display. Everything I insert here is going to be double checked by myself and again by Ben when he comes back from his walkaround.

Halfway through my MCDU set up, John pops his head in to tell me that all the passengers have disembarked. I reach up and switch the APU off. Most airports have restrictions on how long before and after a flight you can have an APU on, and it tends to sit around the ten minute mark for short-haul aircraft. APUs are loud pieces of equipment, which, similar to using maximum reverse thrust, will get on the nerves of residents near the airport, so we only use them when we need them. As the APU spools down, the aircraft is now solely relying on the ground power unit for its electrical supply.

As John squeezes out the flight deck, in a hurry to get on with his tasks, a new face comes in. She's wearing luminous orange shorts and a bright jacket. It's our Spanish turnaround coordinator, who introduces herself as Maria and greets me with a kind smile. She passes me our load sheet for the next flight, informing me that we've been given a slot back to London in an hour from now.

I try to hold a genuine smile in return as I thank her for the not so great, but highly expected news. It means all the work we did to save a few minutes on the inbound flight has now been undone.

We exchange a few moments of small talk before she leaves to supervise the baggage handlers and service vehicles beneath the aircraft. As she does, I notice the latest weather report has printed. I input this data, along with the load sheet data, which gives us accurate passenger and baggage weight & distribution figures for the flight home, into my iPad's performance modules.

I then pause everything I'm doing in the flight deck and decide to take this opportune moment, while we have no passengers on board, to go down the back of the cabin and check in with the crew. It's so easy to end up going a whole day without even seeing the crew down the back. It's also easy to spend the whole turnaround sat in the seat in the flight deck getting sucked into all the various tasks. I actively try to avoid falling into either trap.

As I walk down the cabin, I see that the crew are working hard. To save both time and money, we don't have cleaners who come on board every turnaround. We do overnight, but during the day, it's part of the cabin crew's duty to tidy the cabin between flights and make it look presentable to the next load of passengers. Each of the four crew members have designated rows in the cabin that they're responsible for tidying, and they're blasting through them at speed. They know the faster they tidy, the faster we can get the passengers on and hopefully the faster we can get home.

I check in with each crew member individually as I progress down the cabin, while trying not to distract them too much from their job at hand. They continue to tidy as we interact, but I do believe they appreciate it when the pilots make the effort to come out and check in with them. As I walk, I help pick up some larger items of litter and place them into the rubbish bags left in the aisle by the crew.

I haven't seen or heard from the two girls at the back since the brief over three hours ago, and may not do for the next three hours, so it's potentially the only real opportunity for me to build a little rapport but also check that they're still fit to operate.

After satisfying myself that both the girls are happy and having a nice day so far, I head back towards the flight deck, this time dragging the walk out for as long as I can. This is the first time I've walked further than two meters since I finished my walkaround this morning, and it'll likely be the last for a few hours. My legs need this stretch. I'm extremely active, so the sedentary side of the job is an aspect I really struggle with. We can be strapped into our seats for up to 5-6 hours at a time on longer flights, only able to move when we need to come out to the toilet. I really don't think it's healthy!

As I approach the front of the cabin, I notice that Joel, who's responsible for changing the front toilet bin, is still doing his rows. I'm confident that I'm mostly there with the set up in the flight deck, and I want to play a part in helping the cabin crew, so I elect to grab the toilet bin and change the bin bags over for him. Some pilots do this, others outright refuse and say it's just not part of our job description. I can see it from both sides, but if I have time, I'll do it. The crew always seem very appreciative when you do so. It only saves them around 30 seconds, but every second counts in this game, and it once again breaks down the barriers between pilots and cabin crew.

With the bin changed, I make my way solemnly back into the flight deck and re-take my seat. I can now see our next load of passengers walking down the glass jet bridge, led by the dispatcher, who'll stop them at the main aircraft door. We're not ready for boarding until the cabin crew have completed their duties, but having the passengers queued up ready for when we are, saves time. It's slightly distracting all of a sudden to have passengers peering through the flight deck windows and watching me complete my preparations, but it's all part of the job, I guess!

In some hot countries without air-conditioned jet bridges, I feel extremely sorry for our passengers who are made to follow this procedure, only to then sometimes end up stood in a roasting hot jet bridge for ten minutes or more. I've been known on occasion to tell dispatchers to ignore that standard way of doing things and hold the passengers in the air-conditioned gate if the jet bridge is uncomfortably hot. Alicante is a well-equipped airport though, and the jet bridges are nice and cool.

As I bury my head back into the MCDU, tapping away to insert our engine-out departure procedure, Ben returns from his walkaround announcing that everything looks good.

"Cabin tidy complete, are we ok to board?" asks John while sticking his head into the flight deck as Ben sits down. I give the thumbs up and hear a "let's get 'em on!" as John signals to the dispatcher to release the passengers.

As the steady flow of passengers and repetitive greetings happen behind us, Ben and I are hard at work, still with many tasks to complete if we're to depart on time. Although we have the slot, we're still expected to be ready to pushback at our normal time. The slot can change or get cancelled before we even get to that time, so it's no excuse to slack. Alicante ATC may want us to remote hold as I discussed during the previous departure, in which case we'd still need to push back from stand at our scheduled time.

I've now completed my initial round of setting up the MCDU, so while Ben's calculating his weight and balance figures, I take the opportunity to crosscheck what's in the box with what's on our flight plans and expected departure plate. Our flight plan shows we're expecting the MITOS3A SID departure, so I've programmed this in. Our chart says this SID has an initial stop altitude of 5,000ft, so I dial that into the FCU.

As we've now got around 30 passengers on board, I push the 'Cond' button on our systems display so I can see what the cabin temperatures are. There are three temperature sensors inside our aircraft, one in the cockpit, and one at either end of the cabin. The rear of the cabin always warms up faster than the front, so it's often nice and cool in the flight deck, while it's uncomfortably warm in the cabin. The only way for pilots to see this is to check on our system display.

One of my absolute pet peeves when I'm flying as a passenger is when I'm sat in the back of an unnecessarily hot and sweaty cabin, because the pilots sitting in the cooler cockpit haven't had the capacity to look at the temperatures down the back and switch the APU on.

I'm always conscious of continuously checking the cabin temperatures, as shown on our ECAM screen, and starting the APU as soon as they start to rise. Today, the temperature down the back is already up to 24 degrees, so I reach up to start the APU, knowing that the cabin temperature will likely increase another degree or two before the APU fully spools up to provide cool air.

Ben puts his freshly inked load sheet back onto the central pedestal to indicate he's finished his initial calculations. I crosscheck his scribbles with the numbers my iPad produced. It's a perfect match. My call of "weight and balance validation" indicates to Ben we're about to start the same process we did back in London.

Halfway through the procedure, we're interrupted by more banging on the right hand side of the fuselage. Ben looks down before calling out a figure, "7110". Without needing to ask, I already know this is our uplifted fuel in litres. I'll need to write it in the tech log along with its conversion into kilograms, but that can wait as I'd like to finish what we're doing first. Ben quickly punches the number into the required page on his MCDU, so I know I can find the figure there later on.

We turn our attention back to the weight and balance procedure, and are intermediately interrupted by two people at the same time. Further bangs on the fuselage suggest our attention is wanted outside again. Meanwhile, Maria, the dispatcher, walks into the flight deck talking out loud, before assessing whether we're actually busy or not. "Captain, the gate is now closed so we have our final figures". Ben's searching out the window for the source of the banging as I lean forwards to pick up the load sheet, handing it back to Maria for her to write in any last minute changes. I then see a member of ground staff directly in front of the nose making a big 'T' shape with his arms, indicating he wants to take away the external power connection.

I look up to check if the APU has fully spooled up (to prevent another red-faced moment) before deselecting the external power button on the overhead panel, followed by returning the 'T' signal with my hands to the ground staff. This indicates they can disconnect the power cable from within the front nose wheel bay. We're told that if we don't deselect it within the flight deck before they pull it out, it could cause an electric shock to them. On many occasions, however, I've had groundcrew yank it out without asking us to deselect it first, and unless they were really good at covering up receiving a severe electric shock, they seemed ok.

I look up at the guidance board, '-8' now. The last 22 minutes have flown by. I quickly weigh up whether to use this moment of silence to begin our process of inserting and crosschecking the take-off performance figures into the aircraft's computer, but as the dispatcher's just about to hand back the load sheet, I'd rather prioritise finalising her figures so she can leave the aircraft, as we can do the performance figures once she's gone without delaying the closing of the main door.

Before she can leave, she'll need that pink slip from my tech log, so as Ben starts plugging the new changes to the passenger and baggage figures from the amended load sheet into his iPad, I grab the tech log and write in the uplifted fuel figure, running the conversion calculations on my phone calculator as I do. I once again check the oil levels in each engine on our systems display, before signing off that I'm happy to accept the aircraft on this sector.

Ben holds up his newly completed load sheet next to his iPad calculations, and I compare both of them, reading them aloud as I do. All looks great to me. I take the load sheet, give it my final signature, checking that the dispatcher's signature is also on it, before ripping the pink copy from behind it to give to Maria, placing the top copy, which we'll keep, on my tray table that I have pulled out in front of me. The tray table, in my opinion, is one of the finer features of the Airbus. Our counterparts who fly Boeings don't get such a luxury. Instead, they have to contort themselves around the flight controls when wanting to eat, write, or do anything that requires them to place something in front of them.

I rip the pink copy out of the tech log to hand to the dispatcher too, before stowing the book behind me. That's the paperwork all done now. We both thank Maria for her efficient turnaround and wish her a lovely day, before turning our attention once again back to the weight and balance entry procedure. Third time lucky.

The last few passengers are just boarding, so I know we'll only have a minute or so before we get interrupted again. We finalise the weight and balance figures in the aircraft's system before running through the performance validation procedure, inputting the take-off speeds from our iPads into the aircraft. Seconds later, John pokes his head into the cockpit. "Boarding complete, happy to close the main door?". I give him the nod, as Ben announces he'll get the ATC clearance for our departure.

Alicante, unlike London, requires us to call on a radio frequency to get our departure clearance. It's more of a pain than doing it digitally as these clearance frequencies, otherwise known as 'delivery', are usually busy. Clearances are long and include the runway you're cleared off, the departure, the airway, the latest QNH, and a squawk code. This must all be read back in full, so you can end up spending a fair amount of time waiting on the frequency trying to get yours. Digital Clearance (DCL) is definitely the way forward, it just takes investment from the airports to enable this facility.

Today it's relatively quiet, so we're given our clearance quickly. As they verbally deliver each part, I'm checking that it's what we've prepared for. "Cleared for the Mitos three alpha departure, initial climb altitude 6,000ft, QNH 1015, squawk 6544, slot 11:05". Ben reads it all back as he inserts the squawk code into the transponder. I then call out "6,000" while pointing to the pre-set altitude displayed on my PFD, and confirming that the MITOS3A is the departure in the box.

'-3' displays on the guidance screen now, but our slot time is still around 25 minutes away. Pushback and taxi can take 10-15 minutes, so I'm anticipating a ten minute delay on stand. I ask Ben to inquire with ATC whether they'd like us to push to a remote hold. ATC inform us they don't need our stand for another aircraft, and they'd like us to absorb the delay while still sat at the gate. With a delay as short as this, it actually makes life easier for us to do this.

Once again, the ground intercom crackles to life. "Flight deck from ground, hello?" It's our same lovely dispatcher, confirming that all her checks are complete, and the jet bridge is just being removed. I ask Ben to send a ready message to ATC. However, I'm sure it won't make much difference today as we're only going to be waiting here for ten minutes anyway.

Ben and I haven't had time to brief yet, but as it's quite a standard airport and departure that we've both done before, I opt to speak to our passengers first. Although it's lovely to welcome passengers on board with a PA, and nice for them to hear from the pilots before we depart, I'd never delay a flight for it or prioritise the PA above anything to do with operating the aircraft safely, i.e. a thorough departure brief if needed.

If we were much tighter on the slot, I'd prioritise the on-time departure and do my PA once airborne, explaining the reason for not doing one on the ground. Today, however, Ben and I will have time to do our departure brief after the PA. If we don't push back at the expected time and are sat stationary on the stand, passengers will probably start to wonder what's going on.

I pick up the PA phone and greet the passengers with the usual speech, adding an explanation about the slot, which has now become part of the normal routine. John pops his head in as I'm halfway through, silently waving his hands around in a closing motion to ask if he can close the cockpit door. The sooner they close us in, the sooner they can start their safety demonstration to the passengers. Another thumbs up comes from me as I wrap up my spiel to the passengers. As soon as I'm done, it's time for the departure brief.

We take five minutes running through the same briefing format as we did in London, before running the same checklists. As we do, we receive a call from ATC. "Slot improvement, 10:58, contact ground on 130.655 for push and start". Super! How cynical of me to think it wouldn't improve.

We run through the last few items of the checklist that was interrupted by ATC's call, before Ben tunes the ground frequency and requests push and start clearance. I can hear the safety demo hasn't started in the cabin yet, so I do a very quick PA telling everyone the good news. We're cleared for an immediate pushback by the ground controller, so I release the park brake and we're away!

Return Departure

I won't go into masses of detail about the return departure, as quite frankly, it's a carbon copy of that out of London, just with me at the controls and Ben as PM. I elect to hand fly the first few turns on the departure as it's a beautiful day in Spain and there's not much traffic around. The departure from runway 10 is always a pretty one here. Seconds after lift-off we cross the coastline of the Costa Blanco, and head out over the Mediterranean Sea, before making a left turn to track up the shoreline.

Around 30 minutes after we depart, we're levelling off at FL350. We're slightly heavier on the way back than we were on the way down, so although we plan to eventually climb to FL370, our aircraft is simply too heavy right now to safely sit at that altitude. As well as the aircraft telling us its maximum safe flight level based on its current weight, we can start to see indications as we get close to it.

The gap between our stall speed and overspeed markers on our PFD is getting rather small. If we continue the climb, these limiting speeds will continue to move towards each other and we'll end up in what's known as 'coffin corner'. This is the point at which our stall speed and overspeed limits move so close to each other that if we slowed down a few knots, we'd stall, but if we sped up by a few knots, we'd overspeed the aircraft. It's not a fun position to be in, especially if you end up hitting some turbulence. Instead, we'll sit at FL350 to be on the safe side until we've burnt enough fuel to make the aircraft sufficiently light to climb to FL370.

Return Cruise

The cruise back to London is much the same as the cruise to Alicante. I spend the two hours finding various ways to kill the time, while remaining tuned into what the aircraft's doing along with the ATC chatter. About an hour into the flight, the conversation naturally dries up a little with Ben, and we both turn to do our own things. I've brought a kindle for when I run out of newspapers, but quite often, when I'm tired, reading a kindle can actually increase my level of tiredness rather than reduce it. Later in the book, we'll explore the topic of fatigue and ways we mitigate this. On today's flight, I don't feel tired enough to use a tool we call 'controlled rest' which is where one pilot will take a nap in their seat. To help keep me alert on this occasion, however, I decide to request a toilet break halfway through the sector. Often getting up and moving around can really help.

A few minutes of social interaction with the crew in the front galley does the trick. When I return to the flight deck I feel suitably refreshed, although I remain on my feet for another five minutes, standing directly behind my seat. I can't stand up straight in here so it's more of a slouched position, but it's nice to do something different with my body than being sat down.

Return Arrival

Overhead Nantes, in the northwest of France once again, this time flying northbound rather than southbound, I begin setting up the aircraft for our arrival back into London.

This is an arrival I've done hundreds of times in my life, so my fingers move fast through the MCDU's pages. I alter a few constraints in the arrival flight plan and delete a few waypoints that I know we won't be using. I quickly check the dates on the briefing charts on my iPad; they're still the ones from a few months ago, so no need to review them for new changes. Every few months or so, the charts are updated or amended. When this happens, we need to ensure we've read the updates.

Once I've completed my set up, Ben has a look through the box and gives me the thumbs up. Despite the fact that we both fly arrivals into London at least once every day of our working lives, we're still expected to conduct an approach brief. Back in the day, "standard arrival" used to be the entirety of the brief from some captains when returning to home base. After a history of incidents during approaches where crews got complacent, management now requires us to brief every single approach thoroughly.

Today, I don't want to teach Ben to suck eggs, but I do want to ensure he's sharing the same mental model as me for the approach, so he can speak up if something isn't going as I expected it to.

I'd like to do some manual flying as it's a nice day, so I focus my brief mainly on the 'how to' part, i.e. exactly what level of automation I plan to use at which stage, and when I want to configure the aircraft. I explain that I'll make the final call about whether to manually fly the aircraft once we're closer to the airport and better able to judge how busy things are.

We discuss the main threat today as being me manually flying the aircraft, and the reduced capacity this could bring us. I explain to Ben that if at any point he becomes unhappy with me manually flying or feels overwhelmed or overworked, he must speak up, and I'll re-engage the autopilot. I promise to do the same if I feel like my capacity is being reduced beyond a certain point too.

A quick PA from me with a final update to the passengers, and we begin our descent down to FL130 as cleared by London. The views are absolutely stunning today. As the nose pitches down, we're still over the northern coast of France. Out to the left, I can see the Channel Islands of Jersey and Guernsey. The visibility is so clear today that as I look forwards across the English Channel to the south coast of England, I can see the white cliffs of Dover in the distance off to the right and can see all the way along the coast down to Plymouth to the west. Seeing such vast views like this always brings a smile to my face, even when I'm now starting to feel the effects of getting out of bed at 3:45 am.

Ben and I put our headsets and shoulder straps on as we commence the descent. Today's approach takes us just to the east of the Isle of Wight, then along the south coast overhead Worthing, Shoreham and Brighton, before making a turn northbound for our final approach into London. Throughout the approach, we're interacting with ATC, changing our flight level and speed, while also enjoying the views out the windows. As we approach Brighton, I'm looking at my navigation display to see if there's a swarm of TCAS symbols overhead our next waypoint. That waypoint is where we usually have to enter the airborne hold if we arrive at a busy time and ATC need to delay our arrival. Sure enough, it looks like there are four or five symbols on the nav display all going around in circles about 20 miles in front of us. This means we can almost certainly expect to hold, so I reduce our rate of descent. We're now in no rush to descend as we can do so while in the hold.

As we're now under radar control with London, ATC will essentially be flying the aircraft through us. They'll be telling us the exact speed they want us to fly as well as which altitude and which heading they want. They give us an instruction to reduce our speed to 220kts while still 15 miles away from the holding waypoint, giving us a further indication that we're likely to be entering that hold. As I bring the speed back, I ask Ben to make the PA to secure the cabin for landing.

Once we've changed over to the next London frequency, they instruct us to join the airborne hold, noting that we should expect to remain in it for around ten minutes. This is commonplace for us in summer, so we'd allowed fuel for it back in Alicante. I input the hold into the MCDU and the aircraft confirms it'll enter it. Hold entries used to be a very complex manoeuvre. You had to conduct one of four different entry patterns depending on which direction you were approaching the hold from. It took up lots of mental capacity and was easy to get wrong. Thankfully, our clever aircraft works it all out for us now and with the simple push of a button, I know the aircraft will enter itself into the hold with the correct joining procedure.

I have a quick check of our current fuel on board. I minus our final reserve fuel and alternate fuel from that figure, verbalising that the amount remaining gives us around 15 minutes in the hold before we would need to make a diversion decision regarding fuel.

If we did end up holding for the full 15 minutes, we'd have to make a call; we could immediately divert to our alternate airfield, which would mean we'd use our diversion fuel to arrive safely at our alternate landing aerodrome. Alternatively, if certain requirements are met, which they are today, we can choose to 'commit' to our intended landing airport. This means we do away with our alternate airport as an option, and instead, we burn the fuel that would have gotten us there, while still in the hold next to our intended destination. One of the conditions required to be able to 'commit' and burn into this alternate fuel is that our intended airport has two separate runways, meaning we'd be able to land even if one of them becomes blocked. We must also have been given an estimated arrival time.

Even with those requirements satisfied, it's the captain's judgment call whether to commit or not. If we choose to commit and then the airport completely closes, or we receive a further delay, we could use our final reserves to get us to an alternate airfield, but we'd be calling a 'mayday' as we do so. That's not a nice situation to be in so the decision to commit is never taken lightly.

Today however, as there's no severe weather in the area and our delay is purely due to busy airspace, we plan on committing to landing at our intended destination even if our hold was extended beyond 15 minutes.

I do a quick PA to the passengers, explaining to them why we're starting to fly around in circles, and point out a few interesting landmarks and towns around us for them to look at. I find it always helps kill time for passengers when they can look at places they're familiar with from above.

As we circle the hold, we also descend in what's known as the 'stack'. The stack is where aircraft enter the top of the hold, in our case today at FL100, and will leave the hold at around 6,000ft to commence their final approach. There will often be a plane circling every 1,000ft, stacked on top of each other. Each plane drops down 1,000ft when the one at the bottom of the stack leaves the hold to make their approach. There are some spectacular views available when you're going around a hold with an aircraft 1,000ft directly above and another directly 1,000ft below you!

Almost bang on the ten minute mark, we've descended to the lowest rung in the stack and are cleared to leave the hold. The clearance is accompanied by a heading and a further descent clearance. So far, I've left the autopilot in as hand flying around a hold isn't that exciting and it's also not the smartest move when you've got multiple other aircraft in such close proximity. As soon as we're clear of the hold, I check with Ben to make sure he's still okay with me doing some manual flying, before disengaging the autopilot and auto thrust, and asking for the flight directors to be turned off. I'm now flying the thing like a light aircraft.

As ATC give us new descent clearances along with speeds and headings to fly, Ben dials them into the FCU as I manoeuvre the plane manually towards them. My visual scan rate across the instruments is rapid, and I never focus on one thing for more than a few seconds.

I'm aiming for a constant descent approach (CDA), essentially avoiding flying the aircraft at a level altitude at any point during the approach. Although the CDA's been interrupted by entering the hold, I do my best to keep the descent constant for the rest of the approach, avoiding level offs while keeping the aircraft as high as we comfortably can. CDA's are all to do with fuel saving and efficiency, so we don't *have* to do them, but they're heavily encouraged.

To help me figure out a suitable rate of descent, I'm looking at our navigation display to see where the other aircraft in front of us are being vectored onto the final approach by ATC. I'm using that reference to work out roughly how many nautical miles we can expect until touchdown, and then I'm using that figure along with the current airspeed, to calculate in my head how high or low we are on our decent profile. I then use those same figures to work out what our ideal rate of decent should be, then manipulate the thrust levers and aircraft pitch to find it, while keeping the speed where I want it.

While flying parallel to the runway but heading away from the airport on what's known as the 'downwind' leg of the traffic pattern, ATC instructs us to reduce our speed to 180 knots. Moments later, we're directed to make a 90-degree left turn towards the extended centreline, entering the 'base leg' of the approach.

Tasks like this require a lot of capacity and coordination while hand-flying. I'm now turning the aircraft to line up with the new heading, while reducing the thrust in order to comply with ATC's speed reduction order. During the turn I'm also trying to maintain the same rate of descent, as we begin to configure the aircraft.

As we pass through 200 knots, I call "flap 1". I monitor Ben's hand in my peripheral vision as he moves the flaps lever to its first position, while I'm still focusing on the aircraft's trajectory. We've been given the base turn slightly earlier than I expected, which has resulted in us being a little bit higher on the approach profile than I want to be. To correct for this, I reduce the thrust all the way back to idle, pitch the nose down, and ask Ben to extend the landing lights for a little more drag. I know I've got the spoilers at my disposal too, but they're not necessary just yet.

I take a glance out my left-hand window, focusing first on the runway in the distance, then straight down below us. We're flying directly over the village in which I grew up. It takes me a split second to locate my old house as we do. It's always a pinch myself moment when I fly over 'home' while hand-flying an A320 at low level. I used to spend my childhood years there, looking up in awe at the aircraft making their turns onto final approach. Now I'm the one sitting up there looking down. It's a nice thought, but one that can't take up too much time right now as there are other more important things to focus on.

ATC give us another heading that will put us on a trajectory to intercept the lateral localiser beam of the ILS. The speed is now approaching the 180 knots that they asked for, so I pitch the nose of the aircraft down even further to stop the speed reducing through the target speed, which also helps us descend more rapidly and gets us nicely back on our ideal descent profile.

We're now pointing directly towards London. The slight pitch down of the aircraft's nose has revealed an incredible view of the city. In the distance, I can clearly see the clusters of skyscrapers, with the Shard standing proudly above them all.

As I shift my gaze closer, the M25, London's iconic ring road, snakes its way across the vast green landscape below. From this vantage point, we can see countless other roads and motorways branching off, weaving an intricate network across the countryside.

 I take another look to the left at the runway as it starts to come into clear view now. The visual picture and aspect of the runway reflects what our instruments tell us: that we're on the correct descent profile and rapidly approaching the localiser beam from the south. The beauty of hand flying on such a clear day is that I can anticipate the final turn to line up with the runway before the instruments suggest I need to. I begin a nice gentle turn to roll out on the extended runway centreline, still 12 miles out from the airport. As I do, I'm scanning the vertical glideslope indicator on my PFD which is now sitting ever so slightly above where it should be. I request the selection of flaps 2. Ben acts on the request and we feel the aircraft balloon up slightly as the flaps deploy, creating a burst of extra lift. I counteract the balloon by nudging the nose down further, but not too much as I actually want the balloon to push us upwards so we can capture the glideslope.

With no flight directors on my PFD, there's no cross hairs telling me where I should be pointing the nose of the plane to stay on the ILS path as we descend down it. Instead, I scan the ILS indicators, along with a little symbol on my PFD called 'the bird'. The bird is a small symbol that shows us our 'track', i.e. the aircraft's trajectory, accounting for any deviation due to wind. If I'm on the ILS glideslope and localiser, I can simply move the sidestick until the 'bird' symbol is lined up laterally with the runway track, and vertically with a three degree descent angle. This trajectory should keep us nicely on the correct path as we descend. Using the bird makes life a lot easier when hand flying, but I still have to scan all our other instruments and parameters, including our rate of descent, thrust setting, airspeed, etc.

The rest of the aircraft configuration happens exactly how it did down in Alicante, and I also opt to do a flap 3 landing. In the final few hundred feet before touchdown, my level of focus increases further. We have a very small tolerance on either side of the airspeed that we need to hold during the final stage of the descent to still be classed as stable. If the speed is allowed to move outside of these parameters, we'll have to do a go-around. When the auto thrust is engaged, it does a superb job of keeping the speed within the tight tolerance. Today however, it's my left and right hands that'll be trying to keep the speed within those tolerances.

At this stage I also have to turn more of my attention outside the window onto the fast-approaching piece of tarmac that we're just moments away from landing on. Too much focus on my instruments inside the flight deck here would lead to me overcontrolling, but too much looking out the window at the runway could lead to our airspeed or other parameters becoming unsafe and me not correcting for them quick enough. It's a fine balance that needs to be struck.

As we pass overhead the threshold and hear "50" once again from the radio altimeter callout. I take one last glance at the speed, our vertical rate of descent, and the wind speed and direction, then focus my eyes out to the end of the runway. All being well, it'll be the last time I'll look at the instruments until we're on terra firma.

Having hand flown the aircraft for the past 15 minutes, I'm very tuned into it which tends to help when 'feeling' the flare and landing. I have all the data in my head regarding our weight, speed and external environment, which gives me a good idea of when I want to start my flare, and the rate at which to do so. At around 25 ft, I start the process. My eyes are already looking towards the end of the runway, and I use the external picture to adjust my input on the sidestick as necessary. At 10 ft, I add some pressure to the right hand rudder pedal to counteract for the slight crosswind we have from the left, this is known as 'de-crabbing'. As I do so, the front of the aircraft yaws round to the right, lining us up with the runway centreline, but with this comes an adverse secondary effect; the left wing has just essentially gained some airspeed over it as it's been swung faster into the path of the oncoming airflow, which in turn gives it more lift. The opposite has happened with the right hand wing. As we yawed to the right, that wing was sent slightly backwards in terms of the relative airflow, therefore losing lift.

The plane now wants to bank to the right, as the left wing has much more lift than the right. As we're now facing straight down the runway, rather than angled towards the wind, we're also going to start getting blown off the centreline by the crosswind.

I add a small left input onto the sidestick at the same time as I apply the pressure to the rudder with my foot. We conduct enough crosswind landings in real life for this coordinated move to become muscle memory, and they also form part of our simulator training every six months to ensure it's second nature to us. I drop the left wing slightly lower than the right, so we can keep pointing the nose down the runway without getting blown to the side. I make a final few corrections in the last second just as the left main wheel makes contact with the tarmac and continue to fly the right wheel down too. The ground spoilers deploy and initially try to push the nose up, which I counteract by reducing the back pressure on my sidestick. I reach my fingers over the front of the thrust levers to apply the reversers while still flying the nosewheel onto the ground.

I always find it amusing that on a standard day, a pilot's day can usually be defined by the quality of their landing. Our duties are often ten or more hours long, yet the decisive factor for most of how they performed can often come down to the second in which the main wheels touch the ground. There is a lot of skill involved in landing an A320, and a high level of capacity required to absorb lots of information in the final few seconds and translate that to the correct inputs onto the controls, however, some of it does come down to luck. There's not much you can do about a last second gust of wind hitting the aircraft, or a sudden change in wind direction over the threshold causing the aircraft to sink or float.

Today I was happy with my landing, so there's a slight sense of achievement as the aircraft decelerates through 50 knots and I steer us off the runway using the rapid exit taxiway, stowing the reversers and disarming the ground spoilers as I do so, meaning Ben can begin his flow.

We're switched over to ground ATC who give us a clearance to our stand "08 Left, Tango, Juliet, Quebec, Quebec Charlie, 572". Ben reads it back word for word, while in my head I trace out where that means we'll be going to get to stand 572. I've been here long enough to know all the stands and taxiways, but still reach over to select it on my iPad chart for good measure.

We run the post landing flows and as we hit the three minute mark from touchdown, we're still not at our parking spot. This gives us the opportunity to do a single engine taxi arrival; another way we try to save a little fuel and some wear and tear on the engine. Ben points to the number 2 engine master switch, and upon my confirmation, moves it into the off position. On our aircraft, the two engines supply a different hydraulic system each, so to keep pressure in both systems when we have one engine shut down, Ben reaches up to turn on an electric hydraulic pump. This pump makes a distinct sound in the cabin, similar to that of a dog barking. I'm sure more people who've travelled on an A320 would've heard this sound before.

Shutdown

The parking and shutdown procedure is a mirror image of what happened in Alicante, only this time we have a wider smile on our faces. It's almost home time! While the passengers disembark, I finish all the paperwork in the tech log and check everything's been correctly closed and sent off from our iPads. We've arrived slightly behind schedule due to the airborne holding, and as I look up at the guidance screen, it's already changed to the next flight number along with '-40'. Thankfully, we're not operating that flight. I look at our crew sheet to

135

see where that flight's going. It's all the way to Egypt and back. That's a 12 hour day with no delays. I'm very happy to be finishing work right now rather than just starting!

'-40' denotes there's 40 minutes to go until this aircraft is due to pushback full of its next load of passengers. This implies the next crew are likely already waiting at the gate, as they would have reported 20 minutes ago to security. We therefore know we'll likely not be completely shutting the aircraft down as we'll be doing a transit turn and handing the aircraft over to them. As such, I type in the next crew's flight number and destination into the MCDU and hit 'send request'. This isn't SOP, but getting the ball rolling on downloading their flight plan for them can save them some time and it's a nice gesture.

As soon as the last passenger is off, Ben and I would run a 'shutdown' checklist if this aircraft wasn't going straight back out again, but instead start to pack our things away and vacate the flight deck. The next crew are already standing on the jet bridge at the entrance to the main aircraft door. While our cabin crew finishes their duties cleaning the cabin, I jump off and have a quick chat with the outbound pilots. Again, they're two people I've never met before. I let them know we've had no new defects on the aircraft and there's nothing really to report in terms of general issues. We then move onto a bit of small talk about their rosters that week. There's a new policy where the outbound crew aren't allowed onto the aircraft until the inbound crew have disembarked. Something to do with too much chit chat going on between all the crew, and the process of changing over crews grinding to a halt.

I do understand that, but as pilots, we need to speak to the other pilots to inform them of any issues with the aircraft, so we now have to get off to do this. When there's not much to report though, I like to use the opportunity to actually speak to other pilots as it's really the only chance we get all day to interact with another crew aside from our own.

Home Time

After a few minutes, our crew are looking like they're ready to go, so I jump back onto the aircraft and ensure they're all off before I grab my things and head out behind them, wishing the outbound crew the best of luck on their 12 hour day as we make our escape down the jet bridge side access door. It's a five minute walk through the maze that makes up the side of the airport passengers don't see, before we get back to the staff area. It consists mainly of trying to avoid getting run over by various servicing vans, trucks, and carts driving around while also catching up with the members of the crew we haven't really had a chance to speak with all day.

As we arrive at the debriefing point, we remove our high visibility vests and bring up any topics that we'd like to discuss as a crew, before parting ways, potentially never to see each other again. 95% of the time, I have nothing to say here apart from praising the crew individually for a nice day out and asking if anyone has any questions for me or the first officer. If there had been an issue to discuss that only involved one of the crew, I'd usually have spoken to that crew member about it during the day. The 5% of times I've felt it necessary to host a debrief are when there's been a notable event on board. It's always handy to praise crew if they did a good job, as well as try and take away learning points, or ask how we could have better helped them from within the flight deck, should the same situation occur again.

After some events, especially medical events, crew may need extra support and this is where I'm more than happy to extend the debrief for as long as they want, to ensure we can both support them in the moment and also ensure they know where to get further support from should they need it.

Today's gone swimmingly, so there's no need to de-brief. We say our goodbyes and disperse. The cabin crew who've been on their feet all day, tend to turn right as they exit the crew area. This takes them towards the staff bus that will shuttle them to the car park. Unless it's hammering it down with rain, pilot's who've sat on their butt all day tend to turn left and opt to walk to car park.

The walk back to the car park can be a strange one. You're often walking with someone that you've just spent an entire working day locked in a box with. By this point you've probably both run out of small talk or simply can't be bothered to make any as you're too tired and know you're just a few minutes away from getting into your car. I felt that Ben and I got on well today (although Ben may beg to differ) so we have a conversation about things outside of flying on the walk back to our cars. On a day where you and the other pilot haven't found much in common, the walk back can feel like an incredibly long ten minutes!

As we're nearing the car park, we both instinctively get our phones out to check our rosters for changes. It's policy to do this immediately after the debrief so that we can accept any changes that crewing has made for other duties in our block. If we don't, we'll get a phone call from a crewing officer on our drive home.

Sure enough, I have the dreaded notification in bright red when I open up the app. 'You Have Changes'. Damn! In my experience, 90% of the time, changes end up being a bad thing. Tomorrow is my fifth and final day in this block and I was due to operate a Venice and back, reporting at a leisurely time of 7 am, which would genuinely feel like a lay in after this block. I click the notification to see they've taken the Venice away from me and put me on a much longer flight to the Canary Islands. Not only does it report at the much earlier time of 05:30, it's also a substantially longer workday.

The longer flight will mean a slight uplift in pay, however I'd rather pay double the difference for the extra hour and a half in bed! It also means I have to cancel the afternoon plans I'd made, foolishly thinking I'd actually finish work at the time my original roster said I would. In summer, this level of roster instability is very common and definitely takes its toll on crew.

Unless the change violates our hour restrictions, we can't refuse it. The only exception would be to do so on the grounds of fatigue. I'm tired, but I know the difference between tired and fatigued and can tell that I'm not over that fatigue threshold yet. I only ever use fatigue when I believe it's completely warranted, so I begrudgingly accept the change with the click of a button, and wave goodbye to my social plans for the next day.

This is the reality of being an airline pilot operating for a short-haul carrier. While our days off belong to us, our working days are really the company's, to do exactly what they want with. We do have certain restrictions and limitations put in place by the authorities and unions, but as a whole, we really can't ever commit to plans outside of work on any working day.

Ben and I part ways in the car park with a handshake. It's been a nice day, but I know I'll likely never see him again. If I do, it'll probably be in passing where we exchange a friendly smile while both trying to recall which flight we recognise each other from.

By the time I arrive home it's almost 4 pm. Having been up since 03:45 am, the tiredness is now hitting me hard & jumping straight into bed looks ever tempting. I know from experience that's a bad idea. I need to try to fight through the tiredness and stay up until a sensible bedtime. A small nap now will massively impede my ability to fall asleep in a few hours' time, which I'll need to do if I want to get eight hours of sleep in before my 04:30 am alarm tomorrow.

Day 2: Earning Our Money

We've just explored a real life example of a standard day in the life of an airline captain. Although every day brings plenty of variety in terms of challenges, problems to solve, different destinations and new crew, the majority of my days follow the above structure.

Being an airline pilot, however, is voted as one of the world's most stressful jobs. What's so stressful about that day we've just walked through together you may ask? A very valid question. The stress levels during that day probably peaked at around a four out of ten, mostly caused by managing slots and delays. We do also get days that sit at the other end of the spectrum, pushing eleven out of ten levels of stress. It's days like this that earn the job its place on that list.

To show you what one of these days looks like, I want to walk you through the most challenging day of my career to date. This was a day that pushed my skills and capacity as both a commander and a human being to the absolute limit. It consisted of three main events, each of which we'll dissect over the next few chapters.

Last Minute Changes

Commencing the day with a delightful 04:30 am alarm, I followed my normal morning routine and arrived at the airport an hour later. I was due to be operating a Berlin return that day, a nice little duty indeed which should've had me on my way home from work around lunchtime. A workday that short was a rarity, usually the company would add another two sectors onto short flights. I'd made a few personal appointments for the afternoon to try and take advantage of the early finish, which was my first error.

As I started trying to load the flight plans onto my iPad during the walk from the car park to the terminal, I saw a notification about schedule changes. I'd been changed overnight from the Berlin flight to operate to Rijeka. Rijeka?! I'd never even heard of the place! The ICAO airport code on the flight plan told me it was in Croatia, but I had to scroll to the visual map at the back of the plan to get an idea of where in the country it was located. It looked like a small airport at the very north of the country, equidistant from the cities of Trieste (Italy) and Pula (Croatia).

This was a longer duty day than the Berlin, meaning I was going to be unable to make the first of my two personal appointments later that day. As well as meeting the crew, reading through the 65-page flight plan, trying to find out more details about Rijeka, and setting the aircraft up, I'd have to squeeze in trying to cancel my appointment before we got airborne in an hour's time.

With my face still glued to my iPad, I rocked up to the staff security channel to find I'd arrived just behind the Emirates A380 crew, comprising of 22 cabin crew and three pilots. This is unlucky timing. Although I'm technically on time as I'm at security at report time, I've now got at least a ten-minute wait here before it's my turn to pass through. While it gives me time to continue digesting the flight plan, it gives me less time to set the aircraft up and discuss the plan of action with the first officer when I finally get there, already adding time pressure onto the day before it's even begun.

After spending the entirety of the walk through the terminal scrolling through my iPad, trying to find out as much information about Rijeka as possible, I arrived at the aircraft to find five other crew members just as dumbfounded as myself. It turned out we were all in the same boat. Nobody had ever been to, or heard of Rijeka, and all of us had been changed this morning onto it.

I'd never met any of the crew before, so I did a quick round of introductions before diving into the flight deck with the first officer, Jamie, to start looking at Rijeka's airport charts together in an effort to try and build some situational awareness of what we'd be landing into in later that morning. This was absolutely necessary before making the decision on how much fuel we'd like to take.

It turned out Jamie was a very new first officer, having only recently passed his final line check, enabling him to fly with normal captains as opposed to instructors. This already indicated to me that I may have to take things a bit slower as Jamie's capacity levels may not be as high as a more experienced first officer.

Our flight plan was showing thunderstorms forecast for later that day in Croatia. Nothing too horrendous and certainly nothing out of the ordinary for summer, but due to the potential weather and unfamiliarity of the airport, combined with Jamie's relative inexperience, I elected to be PF on the first sector. I asked to take 30 minutes of extra fuel to give us some thinking time due to all of the above. I had a quick look at Windy.com (a superb tool for real time weather situational awareness) which showed storm cells currently in northern Croatia, but they looked to be rapidly blowing through the area with clear skies on the way. Had I known what we were in store for that day, I would've doubled the amount of extra fuel we took. At this stage however, with the information we had, even 30 minutes of extra fuel felt almost excessive.

It was a very busy 40 minutes of setting up and briefing in the flight deck, while the rest of the team got the passengers & bags on board. My full focus was on the operation, however, I was also aware that I now had the personal appointment issue to attend to due to the change on report. It was still before 6 am, so the best I could do when I found a free 30 seconds was to leave a voicemail with the company I had the appointment, and hope it was enough.

During the aircraft set up, we got news of a slot that'll be delaying our departure. The reason for the slot was given as 'ATC capacity enroute'. We made an educated guess that it was the French's fault. Despite their much higher levels of pay than their UK counterparts, they seem to forever spend their summers on strike, causing widespread disruption across the European network.

The slot was for 40 minutes after our planned departure time, and ATC told us they'll need our stand for an inbound aircraft, so at our normal departure time, we were cleared to push back and taxi across the airfield to a remote holding position. To do this, we had to start one of our engines during the pushback, release the tug team, and then taxi using just one engine to our designated remote holding position, before shutting the engine down again. It added a bit of complexity to our morning and required the use of further checklists, but it put us in a better position to take advantage of any slot improvements or cancellations as we no longer need a tug crew to manoeuvre, and we're much closer to the runway.

After taxiing to the remote stand, I coordinated with the cabin crew and made a PA to invite any children or adults up into the flight deck to help kill time during the delay. I always check with the cabin crew to ensure they're happy with this before I do so, as it usually draws quite a response! It often leads to a queue that blocks the aisle all the way down to the wings, so it can add to the cabin crew's workload. This day was no different. We immediately had a queue of passengers wanting to visit, going as far down the aircraft as I could see. Jamie and I welcomed in the first few groups of families and children, letting them sit in my seat and showing them around the controls, etc. While doing so, we received a call from ATC about a slot improvement, so we had to disappoint the rest of the queue and shut the cockpit door to start our engines.

Medical Emergency

After a further ten minutes sat in the departure queue at the runway holding point, it was nearly our turn to go. Just as we were at the very front of the queue, next in line for departure, the cabin interphone buzzer rang. We'd already had the call confirming the cabin was secure for take-off, so I knew it wasn't normal to receive a second call at this time.

Jamie's PM, so he took the call from the cabin. I pressed a button on my side of the flight deck, which enabled me to listen to the call while still monitoring the ATC frequency. It was highly likely that whatever was about to be said was something I'd want to hear, and by listening to it the first time around, it saves Jamie having to repeat it all to me afterwards, potentially saving precious seconds if there was a time critical incident happening in the cabin.

The cabin manager reported that one of our passengers appeared to be on the verge of dropping out of consciousness. The man was apparently sweating profusely and was claiming he's about to pass out, with his eyes rolling into the back of his head. Although hearing that was enough for me to know exactly what my next move was going to be, the FO correctly asked the cabin manager on the phone what they'd like us to do. The cabin manager informed us he's not happy with the gentleman's condition and doesn't want to get airborne with him in his current state. I'm in full agreement, so I immediately ask Jamie to request a return to stand with ATC due to the medical issue.

We had a queue of aircraft directly behind us, so we couldn't make a 180-degree turn on the taxiway and return the way we had come from. Thankfully though, as we were at the very front of the queue, ATC cleared us straight onto the active runway and instructed us to taxi down it, vacating at the next exit which would allow us to make our way back to the parking stands.

I felt the adrenaline starting to pump around my body as I advanced the thrust levers to get us moving. My brain started firing on overdrive. I tried to remain as calm and situationally aware as I could, while also thinking ahead to what the next few minutes were going to entail and what was going to be required from us.

As we rolled onto the runway, I asked Jamie to request with ATC that the airport fire brigade have their first aid team meet us on the stand. We could call for an ambulance, but they often take 20+ minutes to arrive and are subject to security searches before they can enter the airport. The airport fire brigade team consists of trained first aiders who can get to us much faster. ATC confirms the fire brigade will be dispatched, while also asking us for more details of the male passenger to pass onto the medical team so they can decide if they'll need to dispatch an ambulance too.

While we were still taxiing down the runway at a rate of knots, Jamie called the cabin interphone to fetch that information. I was then in charge of taxiing the aircraft and managing the radios - tasks that were usually split between two pilots. If I hadn't felt confident here, I would have asked Jamie to leave the cabin call until later on, but this was our home base, so I knew I'd be familiar with any taxi instructions and that ATC here were of very high quality.

Still, my workload was suddenly very high. As I taxied the aircraft off the runway, I was instructed to switch over to the ground frequency for further taxi clearance. Rather than having to stop the aircraft so I could look down and fiddle around dialling in the ground frequency on my side of the pedestal, I simply reached over to Jamie's side of the pedestal and hit the button to revert to our previous frequency. Ground immediately gave us a positive taxi route (meaning all other aircraft will give way to us) straight to stand 50, via Papa and Lima. I knew where the stand was and the exact routing they'd given us, so I kept the aircraft rolling while verbally accepting the clearance.

For all we knew at this point, the male passenger could have been having a heart attack, so I tried to strike a fine balance speed-wise between getting us to stand as expeditiously as possible, while ensuring it wasn't excessive enough to put anyone at risk. This was my first medical return to stand of my career, so although I remained calm and collected on the outside, on the inside I could definitely feel things going a million miles an hour.

I was aware we had various other tasks to complete before we could return to stand. In addition to having to reconfigure the aircraft, we'd have to ensure we started the APU so we could switch off the engines as soon as we arrived. I reached up and did so, before also turning the weather radar off so we didn't fry any ground staff as we turned onto the stand. I decided I'd leave the rest of the after-landing flow to Jamie once he was off the phone to the cabin manager and back with me.

As we approached our stand, it became apparent there was nobody waiting there for our arrival. We're not allowed to turn onto the parking stand unless we have parking guidance or a marshaller, so Jamie immediately informed ATC about our predicament, and are told there was a marshaller en route.

Given we'd only started our return to stand a few minutes prior, it was understandable that there were no ground crew to meet us yet. That didn't take away from how frustrating it was to sit stationary and wait adjacent to our parking stand for what felt like an eternity, for either the ground team to turn up and switch on the parking guidance, or the marshaller to manually guide us onto stand.

At an airport where the ground staff were sufficiently crewed, this wouldn't have been an issue. In summer, the ground crew are a scarce resource and in order to come to our stand, they'd have to leave midway through preparing other aircraft also on tight turnarounds. I used this time to do a brief PA to the passengers, keeping them in the loop and asking them to remain seated even when we stopped on stand. I then asked Jamie to check that the rest of the after-landing flow had been completed.

While remaining at a standstill, we got a call from the cabin manager to say the gentleman's condition had improved. He'd stopped sweating and claimed he was feeling back to normal and already saying he wanted to fly. I told the cabin manager we were continuing with the plan of returning to stand. At this stage, my gut feeling was that I didn't want the passenger traveling.

A few minutes later, a marshaller car came speeding past our left wing. They had to do a ramp inspection to check for debris before they'd turn the guidance on. Thankfully, the marshaller did this at a jogging pace rather than the normal walking pace, before giving us clearance to pull onto stand, bringing us to a stop just shy of the jet bridge.

As soon as we shut down the engines, the jet bridge began moving toward the aircraft. I opened the flight deck door as we finished our shutdown checks, allowing the cabin manager to give me an update on the situation. I also double and triple checked that the doors were disarmed. It's during high-pressure times like this that things such as disarming the doors get forgotten, and then the emergency slides mistakenly get blown when the cabin crew opens a door that's still armed! That's not what we need right now.

The cabin manager repeated the information about the male now feeling completely fine. A big part of me didn't want to go down to speak to the passenger as I knew my human, empathetic side would likely come out and sway my decision on whether to offload him or not. However, I felt it was part of my duty as the commander, especially while we were sitting waiting for the first aiders, to go and speak to him.

I walked down the cabin to find the passenger, easily identifiable by his light grey top that was now mostly dark grey, drenched through with sweat. I dropped down to his level and asked him how he was. He was clearly shaken up, but he was no longer actively sweating. He had his two kids next to him, fanning him, and a wife behind. He explained he had felt faint, but after having some orange juice, he felt back to normal. He wasn't diabetic but thought his sugars were low, and the juice seemed to lift him back up.

As he was talking, I saw a fire engine out of his window, pulling up with its blue lights on next to the aircraft. I gently put my hand on his damp shoulder and softly explained that we were getting the paramedics on board who would do some tests to see what was going on, but not to worry about anything.

The firefighters ran observations on the male for ten minutes while all the other passengers remained in their seats. Meanwhile, I was on the phone to our flight planning team to check if we could still operate out on the same flight plan. All the medical observations came back fine. At this point, I still wanted to get the male off the aircraft, as I felt it was my duty of care toward him, his family, and the other passengers. There still wasn't a clearly identifiable source for these issues, so I didn't want to risk this happening again in the air and having to divert.

I was told by a dispatcher who'd now joined us, that the family had no bags in the hold, so we wouldn't need to open the cargo door or require more ground staff to search the hold for these passengers' bags if they didn't fly with us, avoiding a hefty delay. My gut was still saying to get him off, but other factors then came into play.

The fire brigade manager came into the flight deck to ask me what I'd like to do with the gentleman. I answered his question with a question, asking for his professional opinion on the situation. He explained this was actually a relatively common situation for them. He thought the man's symptoms were likely caused by a mixture of lack of sleep, along with not eating or drinking anything all morning due to the extremely early start. He explained how, as crew, our bodies are used to shift work and getting up at 4 am, but most people aren't, and some struggled to handle it.

My thoughts at this stage were still that he could be taken into the terminal, given time to calm down, eat some food, and hop on the next flight out. When I went back down to reassess the situation and make this suggestion to the family, they informed me they'd already looked at the next flight to Rijeka and it wasn't for another four days. This meant if I removed this gentleman from the aircraft, it would be the end of their holiday. I was now facing two very upset-looking children, along with a worried and frustrated husband and wife. On top of this, I had the eyeballs of almost the entirety of the aircraft on me.

I asked the firefighter who'd run the observations to come with me into the flight deck so I could hear his diagnosis and thoughts on

147

whether the gentleman was fit to fly. His view resonated with that of the fire brigade manager; while he couldn't categorically tell me he was "fit to fly" or confirm the exact source of the issue, he'd be happy with him flying. At the end of the day, it was obviously my call, and they couldn't accept any responsibility for that.

Hmm, decision time.

The FO was already in the flight deck with me and the firefighter, but I now called the cabin manager and the fire brigade manager in. It was a very cramped space, but it gave me the ability to run through all their thoughts one by one. I went around the group asking for their final opinions before making my own decision. The views were heavily leaning toward letting him fly. I then found myself with five people staring at me (the dispatcher's head now appearing in the back of the flight deck waiting to see what he needed to start organising) waiting for a decision.

On one hand, my gut said to get him off. What if this happened again? What if we had to return to stand again? Or, even worse, what if it happened when airborne? What if there was an undiagnosed issue that was going to get exacerbated when the cabin became pressurised? Could I justify the decision to take him if that ended up happening?

If we diverted once airborne, not only could this man end up stuck in a foreign hospital, but it was possible none of the 180 passengers would be getting to their destination, as we might legally not be able to continue to operate to Rijeka and back due to our hour limitations. Was that fair on the other 180 passengers?

On the other hand, I had multiple medically trained professionals telling me the gentleman was okay and essentially fit to fly. If I kicked him off, his holiday with his wife and small children would be ruined. This could be their one holiday of the year.

I thought about which option would leave me sleeping better at night and came up with a plan. I outlined it to everyone in the flight deck, and when I heard no objections, I left my seat and went down to chat with the man one-on-one. I was aware that sometimes anxiety about flying could cause symptoms similar to what the man had experienced, so I asked if he was nervous about flying in general. I informed him that, being totally transparent, there were thunderstorms around the destination, so it might get quite bumpy. If he was nervous, it would only get worse. This was me opening the door as wide as I could for him to get off the aircraft if he felt the desire to. He was already looking much better than when I last spoke to him and was less reserved. He confidently explained to me that he had no issues at all with the flying side of things.

As that was the case, I let him know that I'd cut him a deal and explained my plan. I was going to take a chance on him, but if he felt even the slightest bit unwell at any point, he had to promise me he'd press the call bell. He may know what the repercussions would be, but it was in the interest of his own health and his family, for him to do so.

I could see the relief spread across his face as he realised I was showing an empathetic side and not kicking him and his family off the aircraft. He shook my hand and thanked me, agreeing to the deal. While it was a nice feeling to be able to do that, I knew in the back of my head that if this went pear-shaped, the responsibility of the call to keep him onboard rested fully with me. I'd soon find myself in a meeting with management trying to justify why we took a passenger that we'd returned to stand for. I apologised to the man for the huge amount of attention that had been drawn to him over the past 20 minutes or so, and as I walked back down the aisle, I thought about how I was going to word my PA to the passengers to best inform them of what had happened, without drawing any more attention to the man.

I asked the fire brigade manager what the best kind of food or drink would be for the man, and I was reliably informed that anything with sugar and carbohydrates would be good. I asked the cabin manager to take something suitable down to him, adding that I'd authorise it without payment. At this point, it crossed my mind that this may have been a very long-winded way for the gentleman to get a free pasta pot!

Standing up in front of 180 people at 7 am to publicly speak feels far from comfortable for me, but in situations like this, I feel it's also part of my duty to do a PA from the front of the cabin rather than from within the flight deck. This was probably the first time many or all of these passengers had to return to stand before a departure. Some might be worried or scared, and I think it's important, and hopefully reassuring for them, to be able to see the people responsible for making these decisions, along with me being able to see them when I'm explaining what's happened and why.

I kept the PA relatively brief, informing them that the medical issue had been dealt with and that we'd be on our way shortly, thanking them for their patience and understanding.

I thanked the fire brigade staff, before diving back into the flight deck to try and figure out the next part of this puzzle. As we weren't a scheduled departure anymore, we were out of sequence with the ground crews, which I already knew would mean it was going to be hard for us to find a tug team to push us back. I asked the dispatcher to put the request in, while also making one myself with the ground handling agents' management office using a direct frequency we had. I was told we'd have one there "soon." Famous last words.

Jamie and I had to re-run some performance figures as the aircraft had burned a bit of fuel, so we were a bit lighter than when we'd first attempted to depart. I also had some admin logistics to figure out; as we'd started our engines then shut them both down, we'd technically completed a sector, despite not going anywhere. I got on the phone to our maintenance team who were in charge of the tech logs, to ask them how they'd like me to record this. It was a situation I'd never been in before, even as a first officer.

While I was on the phone, another slot came through for us. The slot was in 15 minutes from now. It'd take us around ten minutes to push back and get to the holding point, so that was going to be tight. We had a ten minute leeway after the slot time where we could still depart, but even so, with the traffic at the hold point we were going to need a tug crew ASAP if we wanted to make that slot.

I completed the tech log and had a quick discussion with Jamie about our fuel. Due to the taxi to remote stand, followed by our taxi to the runway and back, we'd burned through some of our extra fuel. As it was only on the ground with the engines mostly at idle, we'd only used just shy of ten minutes worth of airborne time, so we still had over 20 minutes of extra holding fuel if we needed it for the arrival.

If we decided to refuel here, we'd definitely miss our slot as the fuelling process would take a minimum of ten minutes to top the fuel up to what it was previously. It could also take a very long time to get a refueller in the first place as we were out of sequence. We decided we were happy with the 20 minutes of extra fuel we already had, and handed the dispatcher the new tech log paperwork so he could close the aircraft door.

We then sat stationary on stand for a further very frustrating ten minutes, waiting for a tug crew. Despite multiple calls to the handling agent, we hit the time at which we'd no longer make our slot. ATC told us we'd officially missed that slot and informed us moments later that our next slot was now in 40 minutes' time. Dammit!

I did another PA apologising to the passengers and explaining the situation, just as I saw the tug team turn up in front of the aircraft. After a few minutes, they were all connected up and ready to go. ATC advised us that it'd be a further 20-minute wait on the stand due to the new slot. I decided not to open the flight deck door to invite customers in during this delay, in case the slow came forward. I also felt the crew had already dealt with enough over the last 30 minutes or so.

It was at this point that I realised due to the delay, I'd now be unable to make my second personal appointment later that day. It was still so early that the majority of society was still tucked up in bed asleep, so I left another very apologetic voicemail with the other company. You'd have thought that after ten years, I'd have learned my lesson by now: never try and have a life outside of work on a working day.

Finally, over an hour after pushing back for our original departure, we found ourselves pushing back once again for our second attempt at departing. This time, it went more successfully. As we reached cruising altitude, we made a call to the cabin to see how our gentleman was doing, and the news was positive. I breathed a sigh of relief and reclined my seat slightly. I still ensured we had the latest weather reports for all possible diversion airports on our routing down to Croatia, should he take a turn, but everything was looking good right now. This event alone would be classed as a stressful day out, but little did I know, this was just the very start.

Weather

As we settled into the cruise and finally got a chance to catch our breath, I ran through the usual fuel checks, and then began filling out a mandatory report for the medical return to stand we'd just navigated on the ground back in London. I touched base with the cabin crew regularly throughout the flight to see how our passengers were, most notably the gentleman from the morning saga, and all sounded well. We kept an eye on the weather readouts for our destination, but at this point, it just looked a little windy with light rain reported. Still no sign that there's anything to worry about.

As we flew south of Paris, we heard reports from other pilots of 'severe turbulence' at our flight level on our routing. Our flight plan had denoted *some* turbulence en route, but nothing that would indicate anything close to severe. I was inclined to believe the pilot reports over the digital flight plan, so we opted to drop down to a much lower flight level that, although burned more fuel, was reported to be a much smoother ride. It did mean we were burning even further into the 20 minutes extra we now had left, but the fuel was there for situations like this.

Once overhead the Alps, I began my approach brief with Jamie. We discussed one of the biggest threats into Rijeka as being the high terrain surrounding the airport. As neither of us had ever been, we were unsure if we could expect to follow the approach procedure on the chart, or if ATC would give us headings and vector us onto the extended runway centreline as we got closer. Either way, we studied the strict altitudes we couldn't fly below according to the chart to keep us safe and confirmed we both agreed on them.

Weather was also noted as a threat, but our weather printout was still telling us it was just light rain at destination with no other cause for concern. Since it was unfamiliar territory, I told Jamie I wouldn't be hand-flying this approach and would use a high level of automation for the majority of it. We were going to have enough on our plate trying to descend near high terrain, in cloud, into an aerodrome we weren't familiar with.

I made a goodbye PA to the passengers just before we commenced our descent, thanking them once again for their cooperation earlier and informing them to expect light rain in Rijeka. Passing through FL250 in the descent, we had our first bit of weather showing up on our weather radar screen. Again, it looked like nothing to write home about at this stage.

Our weather radar screen shows a variety of colours depending on the intensity of the water droplets seen by the beam radiating from the nose of the aircraft: Green, Amber, Red, and Magenta. Green is usually just light rain and fine to fly through. We'd often fly through green without a second thought, and passengers may not even notice. Amber is slightly heavier rain, so there may be a few more bumps, and we avoid it if we can. Red we avoid, it could get very choppy and would be pretty uncomfortable in the cabin. Magenta, we avoid at all costs. It will likely be an area of severe turbulence, and it's not safe to fly an airliner through it.

Over the next few minutes, as we got closer to this weather mass, continuing our descent through FL200, it started to paint a slightly more threatening picture on our radar. It was beginning to look like multiple different storm cells were ahead of us and appeared they were interconnected. There were now quite a few areas of amber showing up, but with clear gaps of green between the amber. We asked the cabin crew to secure the cabin for landing now, a bit earlier than usual, so we could ensure everyone would be strapped in by the time we approached that weather.

We were still quite a few miles away from entering any sort of coloured area on the radar, but we were now flying into light cloud, so our visual view of what was going on in front of us was non-existent. We were now fully reliant on our instruments and radar systems.

As we descended further, the radar return started to generate a cause for concern. It was now painting a lot of amber, along with some red patches in isolated areas. There were, however, still clear paths of green even through the worst-looking parts. ATC cleared us to descend to a much lower altitude, but not low enough to get underneath these clouds due to the high terrain, so the current plan was to zig-zag our way through the green bits. Although this may sound insane, it's something we actually do quite often when faced with bad weather. If we can completely avoid weather, we will, but sometimes it's simply not possible. In these scenarios, we request various headings to thread our way through the worst areas while staying in the areas of lightest rain and turbulence. An added challenge today is that we'd have to be extremely situationally aware of our exact position relative to the terrain around us if we were going to be weather avoiding at low level.

I talked all of this through with Jamie as we entered the first area of green on the radar screen, just as the cabin manager confirmed the cabin was secure for landing. Flying into the green was such common practice that I didn't think too much of it. As we did so, however, everything outside went an unnervingly dark colour very quickly. There were a few moments of what felt like eerie silence. Something suddenly didn't quite feel right. I reached up to further reduce the aircraft's speed to slow everything down. As I did, the plane violently dropped like nothing I'd ever felt before. A fraction of a second later, it was aggressively thrown upwards. There were simultaneous piercing screams from the cabin, loud enough to be audible through our headsets and the cockpit door. It was so sudden that I didn't have time to monitor how much altitude we lost or gained in those seconds, but "heck no!" is what my gut shouted. My hand immediately reached out to try and grasp the heading knob. The plane was being thrown around like a rag doll, making it impossible for me to read our instruments, let alone get hold of the knob I needed. When my fingers finally grasped the heading knob, I turned it 180 degrees to the right and pulled it, ordering the aircraft to start the turn immediately.

We would usually ask ATC for permission to turn an aircraft off any cleared route. However, in this case, I'd been building up my situational awareness during the approach and knew there weren't any aircraft around us. I also knew we were still well above our minimum safe altitude (MSA), so we weren't going to hit any terrain by turning. I wasn't going to waste precious seconds asking Jamie to request ATC's permission to turn, then wait for their reply, followed by Jamie's readback, all while we flew further into some of the worst turbulence I'd ever encountered.

My assertive side came out, and I instructed Jamie to *tell* ATC that we were turning northwest. I was fully focused on our PFD and ND to check the aircraft was doing what I wanted it to while continuing the right-hand turn. The screams in the back continued as the aircraft was still being violently thrown around. After what seemed like an eternity, but in reality was about 30 seconds, we finally burst out of the cloud back into some clear air, and it was instantly smooth.

I checked that Jamie was okay, and while doing so, I pushed the altitude knob to stop our descent. That was the first time I'd experienced turbulence this severe, and I wanted to put the aircraft into a safe position so we could calm things down and assess our options. It looked like we'd popped out into a very small area of clear air, with storm cell build-ups now visible out the window all around us.

ATC was on the radio giving us a slap on the wrist and telling us that we shouldn't be turning without their clearance first. Now wasn't the time for an argument or trying to justify ourselves. That could be done later once we were on the ground. I ignored ATC's torrent and simply asked Jamie to immediately request a present-position hold from them, and to inform them we'd just encountered severe turbulence so hopefully any other aircraft can avoid flying into the same area of weather.

A present-position hold would essentially put our aircraft into an orbit in the small clear area we'd found. This was in an effort to give us some thinking time and space to assess our situation and generate our options. It also allowed me to check in with the cabin crew and see if everyone was okay.

During our hold, we reassessed the weather as we made the turns. Our weather radar only shows us what's directly in front of the aircraft, so we completed a full 360 orbit to build our situational awareness of what was happening around us.

It was looking like our approach path to the runway from the north wasn't viable. Our weather radar was now painting a drastically different picture to what it had just before we entered that weather. It was mostly made up of amber, red, and areas of magenta. Jamie and I had a quick discussion about fuel and alternate airport options.

Our choices now were to continue trying to land into Rijeka, or to divert to an alternate airport. We took a quick stock of our available alternates. We had Trieste directly below us. Unfortunately, Trieste is an airfield with very high terrain to navigate, an approach onto only

155

one end of the runway, and today with a stonking tailwind on that approach. Not preferable.

Pula was the next closest airport, but it looked like it was right underneath the storm cells, so we ruled that out for now. Venice was the next closest option. We could see a little bit of weather around Venice out the window, but it didn't look too severe. Our weather radar was also painting the skies above Venice as almost entirely clear. A small airport called Rimini, on the east cost of Italy, was our official alternate airport designated on the flight plan. We could see out the window the path to Rimini looked clear, so I wanted to ensure that whatever we did, we kept that as our main alternate and made sure we had enough fuel to get there regardless of what happened.

Jamie suggested approaching Rijeka from the south side and landing on the northerly-facing runway. A sensible suggestion based on our radar display at the time. Our radar was showing lots of bad weather between us and the airport, but to the south of the airport, there didn't appear to be any weather. There was also a path through the weather that looked much clearer further to the west, which would allow us to get south of the field. We had the fuel, so we designated Plan A as another attempt into Rijeka, Plan B as Venice, and Plan C as Rimini. Having three options made me feel comfortable.

We let ATC know our intentions and requested an approach onto the other runway. They quickly confirmed it and approved our initial heading request.

Usually, ATC gives headings and vectors when you're nearing airports, but as we were the ones that could see exactly where the weather we wanted to avoid was, it was now us who requested headings from ATC and told them where we'd like to go.

As we tracked west initially, well clear of any weather, I delegated and asked Jamie to start setting up 'the box', essentially programming the aircraft for the arrival into the other runway. While he did this, it was time for me to move onto the 'communicate' part of our 'Aviate, Navigate, Communicate' mantra. I called the cabin manager over the interphone to check in. It sounded like all the passengers were shaken but okay. I was informed that one of the crew had hit their head on a canister at the back of the aircraft, but they were fit to continue operating. I made a mental note to go check in with that crew member once on the ground. After finishing the call, I did a quick PA to the passengers for reassurance.

I'd left it until now to say anything, as I don't like doing PAs at a point where we don't have a plan. For me, the priority was figuring out what we were doing, then I could let the passengers know afterward. I kept the PA brief, apologised for the bumps, and explained that we were going to approach from the other end of the airport, which was looking clear of weather.

By now, we were at the point we'd picked out to start transitioning to the south, so I turned the aircraft 90 degrees to the left, through what looked like a much clearer path than before.

More Weather

Within moments of entering the cloud cover, the plane got tossed around like a paper bag once again. My gut instinct kicked in, and I immediately turned the aircraft around without hesitation, again to the dismay of ATC. I could clearly see there were no other aircraft within our vicinity displaying on TCAS, and I hadn't heard the controller speak to a single aircraft since we'd been in his sector so it didn't feel like an unsafe manoeuvre. I told Jamie I was absolutely not trying that again and suggested we go the ultra-long way around these cells to get us to the south of the field. Our radar showed an edge of these cells to the west that looked quite defined. It would add around 60 miles to our approach, but we had sufficient fuel for this, while keeping enough fuel to get to Rimini if we needed to divert.

We let ATC know our plan, and they approved the large deviation, finally giving us clearance to adjust our heading as required (a little too late!). As we started to make our way around the outside of the cells, ATC informed us that military aircraft on the ground had heard about our plan and were advising us they didn't deem it possible to land at the airport due to the approach at both ends being covered with huge storm cells. Our radar still wasn't showing them, but once again, I was inclined to believe reports on the ground over what we could see. Our radar could only penetrate through so much, so it was potentially just not managing to pierce through the thick layer of storms in front of us.

Either way, if the military classified it as unlandable, we weren't trying it. It was now time to reassess our options. We had around ten minutes of fuel available to us, which gave us the option of holding here to see if the weather improved enough for us to make an approach. The wind at our current altitude was quite strong, meaning the storm cells will be blown over and eventually away from the airport. We could further extend the time we'd have in the hold by changing our alternate from Rimini to Venice. Venice was closer, so we'd need less fuel in the tanks to get there. Our other option would be to divert immediately to an alternate airport, refuel and wait the weather out, then return to Rijeka with plenty of fuel in the tanks.

My heart was firmly set on the latter. I couldn't see this weather clearing up in the next ten minutes, and I'd rather end up at an alternate airfield with ten minutes extra fuel rather than being down to our final reserve. Although my heart was set, I presented the options to Jamie before airing my preference. It's always good to ask the FO's opinion before you've influenced it, just to see if there was something you hadn't thought of.

At this point, the cabin crew called. I decided to take this call myself, leaving Jamie to think about which plan made the most sense to him. It was the cabin manager asking if we were okay and wanting an update. I explained we were all good, just heads down trying to sort a plan, and that I'd get back to them and the passengers once we knew what we were doing. Again, nothing worse than a PA from the captain who sounds unsure of a plan. After a short chat, Jamie agreed with my preference to initiate a diversion.

During our earlier orbit, we had discussed Venice as an option for Plan B, as it was much closer to our destination than our flight plan alternate, Rimini. It was also a much better-equipped airfield and one of our airline's bases, which massively helps with logistics once we're on the ground. The weather around Venice looked clear on our radar screen from where we were, and the previous weather reports had been okay, so we requested the diversion there with ATC and pointed the plane toward Venice airport, while still dodging other storm cells. We designated Venice as our new Plan A and Rimini as Plan B.

158

As soon as we were clear of the immediate weather and heading toward Venice, I asked Jamie to take control while I started to set the aircraft's systems up for the approach. I planned to do this and then speak to the passengers once we were all prepared for the approach in the flight deck. As the minutes passed and we got a little closer to Venice, however, our radar screen filled up with a wall of red, directly overhead their runway. When we were finally handed over to Venice's radio frequency, all chaos was erupting on the radio. We heard various calls from distressed-sounding pilots, including the phrases "low fuel" and "unable to hold," mixed with "unable to land due to weather." I didn't fancy joining that party.

Without the time for debate, it was time to pull the trigger on what was now our Plan B: Rimini. I'd never been there, and it was a little further away than Venice, but on our radar, it looked clear. Even more importantly, I could physically see the east coast of Italy out the window to confirm it was clear of weather. The weather report was reading calm winds and clear skies, so we pointed the plane in that direction. Jamie got a word in edgeways with Venice ATC when he could, which was a check-in and diversion request all in the same message. I wonder if that was a new one for them!

During the 20-minute flight to Rimini, I handed control to Jamie once again to free up my capacity. I did a PA, letting our passengers know we were diverting to Rimini and would assess the situation once on the ground. I promised them more information later on, but for now, shared that it was likely this would just be a refuel stop, by which point the weather would have blown through Rijeka, and we'd be able to make the short hop back over there in clear weather. I then set the box up for the approach and ran through a full approach brief with Jamie. I also sent a digital message to our company letting them know we'd be diverting, just to get the ball rolling with logistics from their side.

Then it was time for a final review. The adrenaline had been pumping for both of us for the last half an hour, so this was now an opportunity to take a breath, slow everything down, and share between us a review of where we were at, what our plan was, and essentially double-check we were making the right decision. To do this, I took back control of the aircraft and asked Jamie to verbally run through a review. I find that doing it this way ensures the first officer is engaged and that they fully understand what the plan is.

We were both happy with the plan, so we continued to Rimini. As we entered their airspace, the environment looked night and day compared to what we had been in just 20 minutes ago. Bright blue sky, almost without a cloud in sight. Most of the bad weather was directly behind us and blowing the other way. I could see a few weather buildups in the far distance off to the west that were going to be coming our way eventually, but right now we'd found a nice pocket of very clear air.

The approach and landing into Rimini were standard, and as our main wheels touched down, I felt a wave of relief. The airport was a small one, and it looked like we were the only aircraft there. It had a very tight parking area, so I carefully manoeuvred the aircraft around the taxiways and parked following the marshaller's guidance, before shutting down the engines and starting the next chapter of this saga.

Refuelling

So far today, we'd had a last-minute change on report to a destination that we'd never heard of. After being initially delayed due to a slot and having to manoeuvre the aircraft to a remote holding stand, we'd eventually made it as far as the departure runway before needing to return to stand due to an urgent medical situation.

After the first aiders had done their thing, and I'd taken the decision to allow the passenger in question to fly, we were finally on our way to Rijeka, only to find that the airfield was surrounded by impenetrable turbulence and storm clouds.

After a double diversion, initially to Venice then to Rimini, we'd finally touched down into the quiet airfield on the east coast of Italy. As we were the only aircraft there, and I couldn't see how the day could get much more stressful, I fully expected this to be a simple case of refuelling and departing again into Rimini as the weather started to clear up. Little did I know, this was lulling me into a false sense of security.

Oh, and just a reminder that as a crew, we'd all been up since 04:30 am or earlier.

My initial plan was to refuel immediately, wait for the weather to clear at Rijeka, and make the short hop over to our intended destination before then returning back to London. The wind at 7,000 ft had been blowing toward the east at around 50 knots, so we knew it wouldn't take long for the storms to blow over Rijeka and the nice clear air we'd found ourselves in on the diversion to be overhead Rijeka. I was acutely aware that the strong aloft winds also meant the weather I saw off in the distance as we approached Rimini would be blowing toward us at the same rate of knots. A quick look at the weather app on our iPads confirmed my prediction: there was a large gap of clear skies approaching Rijeka, along with another wave of storm cells approaching the airport we were currently at. It was clear we were going to need to time this right.

Once parked on stand, I did a quick PA asking the passengers to remain seated initially, and letting them know that I'll come out to have a proper chat with them shortly. In the meantime, I opened the flight deck door to allow the cabin manager in, as we watched our welcome party approach the aircraft. It's not the ten-strong team of ground crew we're used to. Here it's just a dispatcher and one member of ground crew, who's pushing a staircase toward the aircraft.

My priority here is my crew, so I took these moments to turn and check how both Jamie and the cabin manager are doing. The cabin manager was clearly a little shaken and explained that there are a few passengers onboard who are understandably in quite a state after being scared by the turbulence. I assured him I'd speak to them very shortly, before confirming that our cabin crew member down the back, who hit his head, is definitely okay.

There was a knock at the main aircraft door, and it was soon opened to allow the dispatcher onboard. As the dispatcher came in, I asked Jamie if he could call our flight planning team and get the ball rolling on creating flight plans for our flight from Rimini to Rijeka. We'd need these in order to operate the flight legally and to tell us exactly how much fuel we'd need for the short hop over.

Our Italian dispatcher looked somewhat frustrated that we'd disrupted his extremely quiet day. I explained our situation along with our plan, saying that we'd like to fuel up as quickly as possible and depart again.

He immediately informed me that he'd get the fuel truck on its way and would just need our final fuel figure once we'd decided on one.

It appeared the poor weather across that part of Europe was taking its toll on our HQ back in London. I could hear the dreaded sound of our company's holding music through Jamie's phone, meaning he'd been put into a queue with all the other pilots trying to get through.

I decided to use that time to go and speak to the passengers. Similarly to back in London, I felt it was my duty to do this from the front of the cabin, rather than from within the flight deck (although I did think they'd probably all had enough of me already today). I took a few deep breaths and gathered my thoughts before walking out and picking up the cabin PA phone. I stood in the front galley, aligning myself in the centre of the aisle so the passengers in the back could also see me.

During my PA, I tried to empathise with our passengers, acknowledging that the turbulence had been uncomfortable and reassuring them that we wouldn't be putting the aircraft back into that weather at any point again that day. I explained why we chose to divert into Rimini as opposed to potentially closer options, along with our plan to refuel and then make the short hop back across the Adriatic as soon as a gap presented itself in the weather, which wouldn't be too far off. I think the bright sunshine streaming in through the windows reassured people that I was being honest and truthful, but I could still see some very nervous faces as I was talking.

I explained that I'd turn the seatbelt signs off while we refuelled, and they were welcome to use the facilities, but I asked them to please keep the aisles clear so the cabin crew could perform their duties.

I immediately made my way to the back of the aircraft to speak directly to the crew member who'd hurt his head. As I did, I got peppered with questions from passengers. I knew if I started answering them then, I'd get stuck there for a long time, so I responded that I'd answer them individually shortly. I sat down in the back galley with our cabin crew to have a chat with him, and was relieved to hear that despite knocking his head on a canister, he was feeling okay.

I then saw the dispatcher boarding the aircraft again at the front and heading into the flight deck, likely looking for me, so I headed back down the aisle. Once in the flight deck, he informed me that the fuel truck would be with us shortly, but the airfield operations manager had requested that, in order for us to refuel the aircraft with passengers still onboard, the manager would need confirmation from our company HQ that they'd read and reviewed the airport's manuals. This was a completely new one on me, so I asked him to elaborate. It became clear that, because this wasn't one of our major bases or an airport we regularly operated into, they'd need an electronic signature from our company to authorise refuelling with passengers onboard. The alternative would be having to disembark all our passengers, who, quite frankly, had been through enough already. The process of getting everyone off and back on, along with their bus ride to and from the terminal, seemed unnecessary and time-consuming, which could be an issue since our gap in the weather to make the flight was approaching. Getting that electronic signature sounded like the better option.

Jamie was just wrapping up his call with the flight planning team, so I asked him to keep them on the line and hand me the phone before he hung up. I asked them to put me through internally to the operations team to save us from entering the queue again and ended up speaking to a colleague named Chris. I explained what seemed like a relatively simple predicament to Chris with regard to requiring the signature.

Chris confirmed they'd previously reviewed the documents, and his manager would be happy to email over a signature. I got an email address from the dispatcher, and Chris informed me that the email was being sent over imminently. This was a process that should've taken just a matter of minutes.

Next, I asked Chris to put me through to our maintenance team on the phone. As we'd been through heavy turbulence, I wanted to touch base with them regarding whether we'd need to have anything on the aircraft inspected. They were very quickly able to review our flight data remotely and confirm that the turbulence hadn't busted any limits that would require an engineering inspection before we departed again. These aircraft are built to withstand extreme forces, and thankfully today, we hadn't actually come close to finding out just how extreme.

As I hung up, our new flight plan came through on our iPads, so Jamie and I got down to the business of deciding how much fuel to load onto the aircraft. We reviewed the plan, and it looked as straightforward as we'd hoped. It was a mere 20-minute flight over to Rijeka, and it did not require much fuel at all. I suggested we put three tonnes extra on, which was almost double the total fuel on the plan. While this may have seemed like a large number, it gave us a nice 90-minute buffer in case we needed to enter an airborne hold for any reason or delay our approach into Rijeka. The last thing I wanted to do was to have to return to Rimini to put more fuel on again - that would've been embarrassing!

We stuck the fuel figure of six tonnes in the window just as the fueller arrived, but it was clear from the way he was slumped motionless in the fuel truck that he wouldn't be doing anything until the airfield operations manager gave him the okay.

At that stage, I was fully under the impression that at any moment, the airfield ops manager would receive the signature and the fueller would spring into action. As such, I turned my attention back to our passengers.

Managing passengers is a large part of the command role, and that day was no different. We understandably had multiple distressed passengers on board. They'd just been through the worst turbulence many of them had likely ever experienced. They'd also just been through a diversion, along with a medical return to stand in London earlier that morning.

I OKed my idea with Jamie and the cabin manager first, before making another PA to say that while we were refuelling, anyone who had wanted to visit the flight deck earlier in the day but missed out, could do so now. This was yet again a great way to kill time for both the passengers and crew and took their minds off the delay slightly. I also mentioned that I'd be making myself available either in the flight deck or in the cabin to speak to people individually should they have any questions about what had just happened.

A queue of children and parents immediately started to form by the flight deck, and we welcomed them in as we waited for any news regarding the fuelling. The first few visits were from kids who were excited and curious. Then we began to get a few older passengers who seemed genuinely shaken up. One woman in particular, was in tears as she entered the flight deck. I calmly invited her to sit down in my seat while I crouched beside her, bringing myself down to her level before trying to understand exactly what was causing her to be so upset.

She told me how scared she was of turbulence and the idea of flying back through it. As I tried my best to offer reassuring words, I had an idea. I asked her to pass me my iPad and showed her the exact same live weather app that Jamie and I had been using. I used the time slider at the bottom to show her what the weather looked like when we had tried to make our approach, with the airport and surrounding area completely obscured by severe weather. Then I showed her what it looked like at that moment and how clear it was going to be in 30 minutes. This, along with trying to be as reassuring and receptive as possible to answering all her questions, seemed to put her at ease. I also took the time to run through all our flight controls with her, letting her move them around and explaining how they worked.

One of the main causes of anxiety among passengers, I have found, is the perceived lack of control when sitting in the back of an airliner. Inviting people into the flight deck, teaching them how we control the aircraft and letting them get hands-on with the controls (which don't actually operate anything on the ground) often helps put people at ease. In this case, it definitely seemed to take her mind off things and made her feel better.

As that lady left the flight deck, hopefully a little less apprehensive than when she came in, I saw the dispatcher arriving back at the flight deck door. "Captain, the signature has to be on the paperwork". He explained that the email from our ops team, stating they'd read the documents, wasn't sufficient. The airfield ops manager was going to send a PDF in an email to our operations department, who then needed to place the signature electronically on the PDF before sending it back.

It would've been handy if he'd elaborated on that earlier! I excused myself from the flight deck, leaving Jamie with the visitors, and stood at the top of the aircraft steps as I called our ops department again. Now it was my turn to join the phone queue. As I waited, I noticed that the build-up of weather in the far distance had already visibly moved slightly closer toward us. Thankfully, the aircraft was parked with its nose facing east, and the weather was approaching from the west. Since it was behind the aircraft, the passengers in the cabin couldn't see it, and all anyone who came into the flight deck could see was the pretty blue sky in front of us.

After five minutes of waiting, I got through to Chris again. I explained the situation, and he assured me he'd get it actioned.

As I jumped back onboard the plane, I was accosted by a group of ladies. Unfortunately, it wasn't in the way I'd have liked. They wanted to get off the aircraft, explaining that their final destination was actually much closer to Rimini than to Rijeka. Either that or they'd fully had enough of me. They had bags in the hold, which would've meant if they'd got off, we'd need baggage handlers and equipment to attend the aircraft and sort through all the bags. It would've caused a huge headache for us and almost definitely delayed the flight. While I couldn't stop anyone from leaving the aircraft if they wished, I used all my persuasive skills to try and get them to stay. I candidly explained all the above to the ladies, again showing understanding that it was likely frustrating for them, but it wasn't fair on the other passengers if we had to delay their departure. I explained that if the delay started to drag on for any reason, I'd see what I could do. They gracefully accepted my points and returned to their seats.

On my way back into the flight deck, I asked the cabin manager if the team could start delivering a water service to the passengers. At low-cost airlines, passengers usually have to pay for any food or drink onboard, including water. In times of disruption, however, we can offer a few complimentary items, one of which is free water.

After 15 more minutes of flight deck visits, I became a little concerned as I saw out the window that the fueller was still sitting motionless in his truck, with the dispatcher standing beside it with just as little motion going on. I excused myself from the flight deck once again, leaving Jamie to speak to the continual queue of passengers waiting to come in and have a look around. This time, I took my high-vis vest with me and headed down the stairs to speak to the fueller and dispatcher.

The dispatcher informed me that our HQ had successfully signed and sent back the PDF document, but it turned out Rimini airport had sent them the wrong PDF in the first place. They had now sent the correct one but hadn't received an email response from our HQ yet. I got my phone out once again and dialled our operations team, sighing as I got placed in the holding queue.

This extremely frustrating game of cat and mouse went on for almost two hours, with all our poor passengers stuck in the middle of it. At every attempt, there was an issue on one side, and due to language barriers and multiple people now in this communication chain, each issue took around 30 minutes to figure out and correct.

In hindsight, it would've been much faster to disembark everyone and refuel, but each time there was an issue, it initially seemed like the fix would be simple, and it would be quicker and far more convenient to sort out the paperwork issue than to get everyone off the aircraft and back on.

During these two hours, I had multiple duties as a captain. As well as being the liaison between our HQ and the airport team on the ground in Rimini, I was also still responsible for the safety and comfort of both our crew and passengers.

Everyone was now late, frustrated, claustrophobic, and getting hungry. While managing all the other moving parts, I made a real effort to regularly check in with all our passengers. Despite being on the phone between departments almost continuously, I made myself as visible as possible to the passengers. I did PAs from the front of the cabin every 30 minutes, updating everyone on the situation. I found that walking around the cabin with the Windy.com weather radar on my iPad and showing passengers that the weather was now clear overhead Rijeka, seemed to comfort them.

I kept the open-door flight deck policy for the duration of the two hours, as there was a nonstop flow of passengers wanting to spend time in there, and it was really helping. On a few occasions, I asked for a couple of minutes of privacy so Jamie and I could discuss things related to the flight, during which time I didn't want us to be distracted by our passengers. Otherwise, Jamie did a great job of entertaining them while I was busy juggling various other tasks.

Flight Time Limitations

As we progressed further into the delay, my mind turned to our maximum legal hours for the day. If everything had gone to plan, we wouldn't have been anywhere near our maximum hours. However, these limits are calculated using a combination of sectors flown that day along with our reporting time. The earlier we started and the more sectors we flew, the more restrictive the limits become. Now, with the day turning into a three-sector operation instead of two, we were working to a lower maximum limit. I became acutely aware that this could soon play a major role in our decision-making.

Some quick calculations, cross-checked with our flight time limitations table, showed me that if we departed at that moment, made it to Rijeka, completed a perfect turnaround, and flew straight back to London without any delays, we would just barely scrape into London within our maximum hours. However, given that the refueler was still sitting in his truck at the time, and knowing it would take him around ten minutes to fuel us after receiving the all-clear, it was starting to feel uncomfortably tight.

We have the option to operate beyond the legal limits set by the aviation authorities, using the tool called 'discretion' but it comes with significant caveats.

Firstly, if we decide to enter discretion, we can operate only up to two hours beyond the limit. Landing even a single minute beyond that two-hour mark would lead to serious questions and my flying licence would be at stake. It's viewed similarly to landing with fuel below the final reserve, a major no-go.

Secondly, all the crew onboard have to agree to operate into discretion. While it's ultimately the captain's call, a single crew member refusing to continue could create significant complications. This might mean operating with reduced crew, which can lead to offloading a few passengers (as we must have one cabin crew per 50 passengers on board), or even cancelling the flight altogether.

Using discretion is something that requires extremely careful consideration. The maximum flight hours are in place for one primary reason: safety. We are human, and humans get tired and fatigued.

Entering discretion increases the risk of fatigue-related errors and reduces the ability to mitigate threats effectively.

Not only does discretion mean operating an airliner beyond regulatory limits, but it also means putting your career on the line to get passengers from A to B. If an incident occurred while operating in discretion, a captain's decision to do so would be put under intense scrutiny, potentially in a court of law.

I've personally experienced a TCAS (Traffic Collision Avoidance System) alert while operating deep into discretion. It had been a 'Swiss cheese' event, which ultimately started with ATC using the wrong callsign, us reading that message back and then ending up much closer to another aircraft than we'd have liked to. I believe that if we hadn't been operating into discretion, and tired to the level we were, the event might not have occurred. Our alertness levels as a crew would likely have caught the ATC error in their radio call to us.

Discretion is never an expectation. Every pilot has the right to not use it. Many pilots categorically refuse to ever fly into discretion out of principle, and there's absolutely nothing wrong with that stance. Personally, I tend to evaluate each situation before deciding.

Despite everything that'd happened so far on this day, I still felt fit to operate. To proceed into discretion, however, I needed agreement from the entire crew. After everything they had already been through, I wanted to ensure they felt capable of continuing.

I spoke to each crew member individually, one-on-one, to assess their fitness to fly and to ask whether they were willing to operate into discretion. Thankfully, every one of them was on board with the idea and willing to go the extra mile to get everyone home.

Flight Planning Laws

The next challenge came in the form of flight planning laws, mixed with the discretion issue. The initially agreed plan with our operations team had been to continue to Rimini. However, around two hours into the cat-and-mouse delay, Chris from operations called me and said the company had changed their plan. Once we had fuel, they wanted me to bring the aircraft straight back to London from Rimini. They wanted us to keep all the passengers onboard, with the plan to overnight them in London and fly them down to Croatia tomorrow.

This news was absolutely gutting. The last thing these passengers wanted to hear was that they were going to be stuck on this plane for another 2+ hours while we flew them back to where we started the day!

I quizzed Chris on the exact reasons they didn't want us attempting another landing into Rijeka. Their reasoning soon became clear: it boiled down to a combination of flight planning laws and us operating close to our maximum flight hours. Ops weren't optimistic we'd be able to land in Rijeka that day, citing that they didn't think we'd be able to get in and out due to weather.

The initial option I suggested was a compromise. We'd load the aircraft with enough fuel to make an approach into Rijeka, and then 'divert' back to London if we couldn't get in. This would give our passengers the best possible chance of getting to their destination that day, rather than not even attempting it again.

Chris explained that flight planning laws dictated that a diversion airfield denoted on our flight plan, had to be within a set distance of the intended destination airport. London was way too far away to list as a legitimate alternate. If we wanted to operate to Rijeka legally, the only way to do so would be to nominate a closer airport, such as Venice, as an alternate. If we couldn't get into Rijeka, we'd have to complete the diversion to our alternate, turn the engines off and back on to fulfil the legal requirements, and then operate the flight from Venice back to London as an entirely new flight with a new flight plan. This was obviously massively inconvenient but, more importantly, it added another sector onto our day, and the extra time taken to divert to Venice meant that even if we left in the next 30 minutes, this plan would push us more than two hours over our discretion limit. It was simply a no-go option, and we'd be forced to night stop the aircraft in Venice.

Although, on the face of it, night stopping in Venice would have been more convenient for our passengers than night stopping in London, Chris made it clear that it would have been a logistical nightmare for the team back at HQ. Not only was it much easier for them to find hotels for everyone in London, but they also needed the aircraft we were on for a night flight that evening out of London. If this aircraft was stuck in Venice with us, they'd need to cancel that flight.

This situation had just taken on a whole new level of complexity. While all our staff and teams back at HQ were absolutely brilliant, I had to remember they weren't the ones on the ground here, directly responsible for the aircraft, passengers, and crew. I was aware of the dangers of the sunken cost fallacy i.e. we'd come too far that day, and we MUST finish the day and get the passengers to their destination, but I was confident that if we could get the fuel onboard as soon as possible, there was a clear gap in the weather where we could land in Rijeka and get back out again.

I asked Chris to hold for a minute while I conferred with Jamie, the FO. I wanted to get his thoughts on the situation before I announced my line of thinking, in case I was getting tunnel vision with my desire to get these passengers to their destination. His thinking lined up with my own. There was a clear gap in the weather that would allow us to get in and out of Rijeka, and it would feel ludicrous not to attempt it. We discussed the consequences of trying and failing, however, and realised that it could be quite costly for the company and could highly inconvenience hundreds of passengers from both this flight and the other flight that night that would be impacted.

Decision Time

It was decision time: concede to the company's initial request and head back to London as soon as we'd fuelled up, or counter their stance and persuade them to allow us to attempt a landing in Rijeka? If we couldn't get in on our first attempt, we'd have to divert to Venice, which was our new alternate. Due to this diversion, we wouldn't be within legal hours to continue back to London as the company wished.

I decided to take a calculated risk and told the company I wanted to try an approach into Rijeka. After what these passengers had been through that day, I wanted to do everything possible to get them to their destination rather than just flying them back to London, which felt like giving up.

I figured the best way to convince Chris was to use data and evidence. This would likely require some thinking outside the box. To make sure we were both on the same page, I asked Chris to pull up Windy.com on his computer (it's worth pointing out that this book isn't sponsored by Windy.com, although if anyone from Windy is reading this, I'm open to it). At least this way, we were looking at the exact same live weather radar. I asked him to move the time slider forward by 30 minutes, then by an hour, so I knew he was seeing the same weather gap I was. I told him I saw no reason why we couldn't get in during that window of clear weather.

After I gave Chris my best persuasive pitch, he told me he needed ten minutes to confer with his manager and colleagues and would call me back. I decided to make the most of that time.

First, I made a very open and honest PA to the passengers about what was going on. They deserved to know the situation. I told them what the company wanted us to do and why, which immediately led to an audible response from the crowd – mild uproar with a mix of frustrated sighs. Then, I explained that I was doing everything I could to change the company's mind and try to get us to Rijeka that day, but I also laid out the consequences if we tried to approach and couldn't get in. It's usually a fine balance that needs striking between how much you should and shouldn't disclose to your passengers. Pilots are very rarely dishonest to passengers, but quite often passengers just don't need to know everything. In this scenario, however, I really felt like we were all in this together, and a full explanation really helped keep the passengers in the picture.

I then stepped back into the flight deck to share my plan with Jamie. We now knew the fuel figure we needed to get to Rijeka along with the fuel needed to get from Rijeka back to London. We added those figures together and put that figure into the fuel load window. If HQ rejected my plan, we'd just have more fuel than we needed for the return to London, which would be no big deal. But if they approved it, we wouldn't need to refuel in Rijeka, which would save time, improving our chances of getting back to London before the two-hour discretion limit was reached, which by now I knew was rapidly approaching.

I also had another first: a passenger handed me a paper note about where he thought we should divert if we couldn't get into Rijeka. In this case, it was Pula, explaining that he knew our airline had ground handling agents there and it's just a short drive from Rijeka. I thanked him for his input but let him know I'd already suggested that to our operations department much earlier in the delay, and they didn't want us landing there due to a company ground contract issue.

Pressure

I stuck my head out the flight deck window to assess the weather behind us. Over the previous few hours, storm cells had slowly moved toward Rimini from the west. Initially, they seemed far enough away not to pose a threat, but as we still sat on the ground with no fuel, dark clouds began to rapidly approach the airfield, with visible lightning flashing within them.

If we were still sitting there when those clouds fully covered the airfield, we wouldn't be able to refuel because of the lightning, and there was a strong chance we wouldn't even be able to depart. I also didn't want to disembark the passengers in torrential rain if we still hadn't received approval to fuel with them onboard. With the weather moving in and more time pressure mounting, it was now or never.

I decided to take matters into my own hands. I dashed a few hundred meters across the tarmac to the airport terminal. By the time I arrived, I felt like I'd been baked alive by the strong Italian summer sun. Wiping the sweat off my forehead, I asked to be led to the management office. Once there, I introduced myself to the manager who had been pulling the strings or, more accurately, failing to.

I then calmly, but firmly, demanded that this issue be resolved within the next five minutes. I told him I wouldn't leave his office until it was sorted. He spent two minutes trying to explain, in broken English, that the correct signature still hadn't been placed on the necessary form. But when I made it clear that their incompetence over email was mostly to blame, and that they now had just three minutes before I started disembarking the aircraft, which would likely take up most of their airport staff's capacity, his actions became more urgent. He grabbed his phone, dialled a number and started speaking rapidly in

Italian. A few seconds later, he nodded to one of his colleagues, shouting instructions across the room. For all I knew, they could have been talking about me (I can't imagine it would've been complimentary), but at that moment, I felt we were making progress.

I resisted the temptation to smile and kept a serious demeanour. A few moments later, he slammed the phone down, printed off the final page of the document, and told me that, if my company agreed, he would let me sign it on their behalf as a one-off exception.

Right then, my phone rang. It was Chris from operations, bringing me even more good news. The company had approved my plan, and they were willing to let us attempt the approach into Rijeka, but only if we departed within the next 30 minutes. If we didn't, we'd have to head straight back to London. Perfect timing. While Chris was on the phone, I shared the breakthrough I'd just had in the management office and asked for his permission to sign the documents on the company's behalf, which he approved.

Let's Go

A quick photocopy was made of the signed document, and I couldn't help but smile. I shook the manager's hand, resisting the urge to ask why this wasn't suggested hours ago. I thanked him for his help and asked if they could radio the fueller immediately to get him moving, stressing that we had exactly 20 minutes before we needed to push back.

I dashed back across the tarmac and up the aircraft stairs, wiping more sweat from my brow after the 300-meter jog. After a quick PA to the passengers, waving the signed document to show them the approval, I dove back into the flight deck to make final preparations so we could depart the second the fuelling was done.

Things started happening very fast. Jamie and I finished prepping the aircraft while the rest of the fuel was loaded. On my way back to the aircraft, I'd noticed that the storm cell about a mile to the west was starting to tower over the field. Time was not on our side and the pressure was on if we were to get out of here before the weather hit.

I briefed Jamie that I'd be flying the short hop to Rijeka since, by the looks of it, we had one shot to land. We'd also be unusually heavy due to all the excess fuel onboard, which would affect the landing characteristics and make it even more challenging than usual.

Departure

The next 15 minutes were a blur of action, completing paperwork, checks, and preparing to push back. The pushback itself went smoothly, and the parking brake was released just minutes before the time constraint set by HQ. I breathed yet another sigh of relief as the tug crew started pushing us back. But as they positioned us onto the taxiway, the proximity of the storm cell to the west became alarmingly clear. The clouds were now directly overhead, and the first raindrops started spattering on the cockpit windows.

By the time we started taxiing, the weather was rapidly deteriorating. The rain was now coming down harder, and the storm cell had drifted into our departure path. As we approached the runway holding point, I asked ATC for clearance to divert from our planned departure track, requesting an immediate turn to the east after take-off to avoid flying directly into the storm. Thankfully they approved the request.

I then made a PA to the passengers, who by now could clearly see the storm building outside. I explained that it might be a little bumpy for a few seconds after take-off as we skimmed the side of the clouds but assured them that we'd been cleared for an early turn to avoid the worst of it. I felt guilty about promising no more turbulence earlier, but at this point, if we didn't go now, we wouldn't go at all.

The tower controller could see we were in a race against time, so they cleared us for take-off before we'd reached the departure holding point. To save a few precious seconds, I decided to perform a rolling take-off. Rather than coming to a full stop on the runway, I gradually increased thrust as we taxied onto the runway. As soon as the nose aligned with the centreline, I pushed the thrust levers forward straight to take-off power.

We accelerated down the runway, my eyes scanning the instruments and the storm cell now swallowing up our original departure path. As soon as the wheels left the ground and we passed 500 feet, I banked the aircraft left. The turn was tight, but we just managed to avoid the cell, our right wing skimming the edge of the storm cloud as we executed the manoeuvre.

The next 20 minutes were busy, but thankfully, the weather cleared as we approached Rijeka, which was completely unrecognisable from just a few hours earlier. The airfield now lay under stunning clear blue sky, nestled in breathtaking scenery, with green mountains rising sharply to the east of the airport.

There wasn't much time to enjoy the view though. My full focus was on bringing the aircraft down into Rijeka on the first attempt. I knew how tight on time we were for the legal limits to return to London, and a go-around here would eat up those precious minutes, potentially costing us the chance to make it back that day.

Given that the aircraft was unusually heavy, I knew it would be harder than usual to slow it down on the approach. I tried to find a balance between reducing speed early to configuring the aircraft, but without unnecessarily extending the flight time.

Once established on the approach, I disconnected the autopilot to get a feel for the aircraft's handling characteristics before touchdown. The adrenaline was flowing again as I reminded myself that this was my only shot to get this abnormally heavy aircraft onto the runway within the touchdown zone on the first attempt.

Despite initiating the flare a little earlier than normal to account for the extra weight, the touchdown in Rijeka was firmer than I anticipated. But the most important thing was that we were safely on the ground.

Once we were parked on stand, I quickly got on the phone with our crewing department. As much as I'd loved to say goodbye to all our passengers, I knew we were extremely tight on time for the return to London. I needed to crosscheck my calculations with crewing to ensure we weren't pushing the limits too far.

I managed to say a few goodbyes to passengers as they left, with a couple of them popping their heads into the flight deck to thank us personally. The gentleman and his family from the medical emergency

176

earlier in the day (which felt like days ago) came in to show their appreciation, which was a nice feeling.

Crewing and I agreed that to get back to London, I'd need to use my discretion to extend our maximum Flight Duty Period (FDP) by the full 2-hour limit. We also had to be airborne within 45 minutes, or we'd exceed the limit in London. It was going to be tight, especially since we were still disembarking.

In addition to checking that the crew were still fit and willing to continue operating into discretion, I needed to confirm that the ground crew could turn the aircraft around in time. We had to be pushing back in 35 minutes to meet the 45-minute window for take-off.

I got confirmation from Jamie and the cabin crew at the front of the aircraft that they were all still okay with operating into discretion to try and make this plan work. Leaving Jamie in charge of the flight deck, I walked down the aircraft stairs over to meet our turnaround coordinator. I explained the situation, and she confidently assured me she could have us boarded and ready to push back in 30 minutes.

Perfect.

Next Challenge

I climbed up the rear steps to check in with the two crew members at the back of the aircraft, confirming that they were also happy to operate into discretion. Once I had their approval, I jumped back into the flight deck to set up for the flight home. The crew did a fantastic job of turning the cabin around ready for the new passengers in record time, but just as the crew notified me they were ready to start boarding, our dispatcher informed me that the water and waste truck had broken down while attaching itself to our aircraft!

After three hours on the ground in Rimini, the onboard toilet tanks were completely full, and our water tanks were empty. We knew we couldn't fly back to London without these facilities. I felt the mood shift instantly among the crew. This felt like it could be the final blow.

Two of the cabin crew now seemed resigned to the idea that we'd be spending the night in Rijeka.

I could see our next 180 passengers queued up at the gate, ready to head home. Despite everything, I was still determined to do everything within reason to make it happen. I quickly assessed our options, dashing downstairs to see the issue firsthand and get an estimate of how long the fix might take. The ground crew believed they could resolve it in a few minutes, but if not, they didn't have any other serviceable trucks on standby. Time for another decision: Should we board now, hoping the truck would get fixed? If we boarded and the truck wasn't fixed, we'd have to deal with a full plane of irate passengers who, after a three-hour delay in the terminal, would then be told they needed to disembark the aircraft they'd just boarded, and spend another night in Rijeka.

The alternative was to wait for the truck to be fixed before we commenced boarding. However, if the repairs took longer than five minutes, we risked missing our latest take-off time.

For me, the crew's needs came first. They'd been through so much already, and I didn't feel it was fair to potentially put them in a situation where they'd have to deal with a plane load of passengers who needed to be disembarked. I decided we wouldn't board until we knew we had a functioning waste truck. It was a tense five minutes, but with seconds to spare, we got the thumbs-up from the dispatcher. Time to move forward.

I made my way back into the flight deck as the passengers boarded. I could hear the cabin manager making announcements, asking everyone to take their seats as quickly as possible. The turnaround team worked at full speed, and we ended up pushing back just in time to taxi and depart.

Departure (Again!)

The flight back was relatively quiet, both in terms of workload and conversation. It was clear that Jamie and I were both totally drained after everything we'd been through that day. It also occurred to me on the flight home that I'd barely eaten since we left London earlier that day as every minute of my time since had been spent dealing with issues and managing situations. I was past the point of hunger but gobbled down a sandwich anyway.

We stayed extra vigilant on the approach into London, knowing we were operating deep within our discretion limits and our levels of awareness would be not quite what they were when we left London earlier that day. We needed to work as a team to ensure we upheld the same high safety standards we would on any other sector.

Landing and Debrief

A final wave of relief came over me when we touched down in London, just minutes inside our 2-hour legal limit. It was pretty quiet in the flight deck as the passengers disembarked. Jamie and I are now almost completely out of energy.

This was one of the first days in a long time where I felt a proper debrief with the crew was going to be necessary. They'd been absolutely fantastic that day, so after all the passengers were off and we made our way to the debrief area (where we usually just sailed through), I asked everyone to stop and take five minutes for a chat.

I made sure to check in with everyone, creating space for anyone to raise anything they wanted to discuss about the day. I individually thanked everyone for their superb work and commitment. They had all gone above and beyond to make the plan come together.

Just before leaving, the crew checked their rosters for changes. As our day had extended hours beyond what it was meant to, we'd all been taken off our planned flights for the next day as we wouldn't have had enough rest hours.

It appeared, however, that we'd all been changed onto various flights starting slightly later the next day, all of which were giving us minimum rest, i.e. 12 hours until we needed to be back in the airport for the next duty. The crewing team would've seen how delayed we were that day, but not have had any idea what the crew had actually been through. I really didn't feel it was fair or safe for our crew to be operating again tomorrow on minimum rest after the day they'd just had. As such, I used my position of authority to speak to crewing and request that they give the whole crew a rest day, i.e. a paid day without duty, to allow them to rest and recover. Thankfully, they obliged without question.

By the time I got into my car at the end of the day, I'd never felt so drained. As I closed the door and settled into the silence, I realised that was the first moment all day where I'd been completely alone, without anyone needing anything from me.

At around 15 hours long, it wasn't just the longest day of my career, it was also one of the most mentally exhausting days of my life.

On the drive home, I called Chris in operations to thank him for all his help throughout the day. He was genuinely touched, mentioning that pilots usually never call to follow up after a chaotic day like this, and it meant a lot to him that I did.

Although I expected to sleep like a baby that night, I was kept awake with my brain in overdrive as it ran over the day's events, wondering if there was anything we could have done differently in order for the day to have gone more smoothly. I also questioned whether the decisions I made throughout were correct.

This pattern of feeling the need to question and scrutinise my own decisions in hindsight is something I've experienced after every significant flying event. Although I think it's important to reflect on events and look for potential ways to improve if a similar situation were to arise again, it can be tough to try and just accept that I've done the best I possibly could. I did once receive some very good advice that I try to consider; "The decision you made at the time, with the information you had, was the correct decision".

During my rest day, I decided to submit a recognition nomination for some of our wonderful crew that day. One for Jamie, and one for the cabin manager who I think did a sterling job and went above and beyond throughout the entire day.

Diary Summary

We've just run through days at either end of the spectrum that we can face when we turn up to work. Thanks for sticking with it! Hopefully, the first day gives you a real insight into what a normal day in the life of an airline captain looks like, while also giving you a good understanding of what we do and why.

I really wanted to include the second day as it shows what can happen at the other end of the scale, when things go wrong. Hopefully, I've accurately portrayed how the job of an airline captain is not only to physically fly an aircraft but also to manage crew, passengers, and various other people and teams while spinning multiple plates at once in very dynamic situations. It definitely has earned its place high up the list of the world's most stressful jobs, but it can be an extremely satisfying and rewarding one when you overcome a challenging day such as this one.

As promised in the introduction, I wanted to include answers to all the common questions I get asked about my job, along with lifting the veil that keeps much of the industry feeling quite secretive. My bet is that the majority of people reading this book are likely considering becoming an airline pilot as a career, so I believe it's important knowledge to share.

As such, in the next chapter I've put together in-depth answers to all those common questions. Enjoy!

How Do Pilot Schedules Work?

A question I commonly get asked is 'How do airline pilot schedules work?' Since it's a sizeable topic, I've devoted a whole chapter to it.

This first part will explain the variety of work schedules available to pilots. The next will focus on flight time limitations and how they work. I'll also explain how the rosters are built, along with how vacation days work, while debunking some common myths along the way. Let's dive straight in!

Commercial airline pilots operate on a variety of work schedules called 'rosters', which can be broadly categorised into **'fixed'** or **'flexible'** types.

A **fixed roster** follows a set pattern of working days. This provides pilots with a predictable routine, often allowing them to have a more stable work-life balance.

In my airline, we operate a 5-4-5-3 fixed pattern. This comprises of five working days, followed by four days off, then another five working days followed by three days off. The pattern then repeats continuously, so pilots on a fixed pattern can tell which days they'll be working in 25 years from now if they wished to! The stability and predictability of a fixed pattern is great for some, but flying for five consecutive days every block can be extremely exhausting. You're also very limited in your options if you need to take a certain date off work in the future, but it falls on a working day. You essentially have to take it as holiday, which is highly likely to not be possible as I'll explain later on.

Flexible rosters (otherwise known as 'random rosters') on the other hand have no set working day pattern. Often, you'll have to wait until the middle of the month before, to find out which days you'll be working the following month. For example, at my airline we'll find out on January 17th which days we'll be working in February. Understandably, this can lead to challenges in terms of planning anything outside of work. While those on a fixed roster will also only find out their flights and therefore working hours on the same date, they'll already know which days they will and won't be working.

One benefit of a flexible roster is that your working days may be spread out more evenly across the month, and you're likely to be doing three or four days of work in a block each time rather than five. Pilots on flexible rosters are also usually given access to various tools to help them build a little more stability into their lives, such as the ability to select a preference for certain days off.

Those just starting out with an airline will often be placed on flexible rosters as this gives the company more freedom to adapt the rosters to the flying schedule. As a pilot progresses with time at the company, they will be given the option to move onto a fixed roster.

Bidding

Most airlines offer a bidding system enabling pilots to select their preferences for things such as early or late duties, certain days off (only on a flexible roster) and specific flights to be operating. It's a way to offer pilots some control over their schedule, but it's only bidding and it doesn't necessarily mean you'll get what you bid for.

These bidding systems are seniority based in some airlines, such as British Airways, whereby the pilots that have been with the company the longest can essentially design their own rosters, as their bid will be considered before anyone more junior than them. Unfortunately, this leaves the most junior pilots with the worst duties and potentially years of 'slogging it' before they can get a comfortable roster.

Other airlines operate their bidding system on a more equal playing field, disregarding seniority and instead rotating which pilots get their bids as a priority each month. This allows more junior pilots the ability to sometimes get the duties and days they bid for, however, the more senior pilots may get frustrated at this system.

In my experience, the bidding system is good, but it's not the be-all and end-all. I often don't get what I bid for, but it's nice to know it's sometimes considered.

Standby

Something I commonly get asked about is how 'standby' works. With major airlines, pilots will often be given 'standby' days, during which they must be able to report at the airport within a set time if they are called for duty (usually 90 minutes). They're free to do as they wish on a standby, as long as their phone is on.

My standby duties usually last between 6-8 hours, but I can get called for almost any length of duty during this time. While getting paid to be on standby can be great, it often means you can't commit to any plans as you never know when you're going to get called. Speaking from experience, you can get called in the last few minutes of your standby to go and operate an extremely long day!

Some airlines will also roster 'airport standby' whereby you don't have a flight, but you must be physically at the airport. It's a way for airlines to cover off any last minute sickness issues or very unexpected delays, during which a replacement crew or pilot is needed immediately.

Private jet pilots will often have rosters consisting mostly of standby, as their flights will be dictated by their clients' needs, which often only become clear at short notice.

To look at a real-life example of an airline roster, please head over to pilotbible.com and look at the blog post on pilot schedules.

Short-Haul vs Long-Haul

Short-Haul pilots can operate between two and six flights each day, often with no time off down-route and just a 30 minute turn around instead.

Long-Haul pilots on the other hand, will often have four or five trips per month. Each trip will consist of a flight out, followed by a few days at the destination, before flying back.

Part-Time Airline Pilot Schedules

Airline pilots can apply for part-time schedules and given the intensity of the job, this choice is becoming popular. Part time options typically include 75% and 50% rosters. Pilots on a 50% roster at my airline will work nine days per month. They only get paid 50% of what a full-time pilot earns, but they regain huge control over their work-life balance. Part-time contracts are popular with pilots who have children, along with pilots who may run a side business.

Flight Time Limitations

Each aviation regulatory body (FAA, CAA, EASA, etc.) has its own restrictions regarding how long airline pilots can work each day, known as Flight Time Limitations. These FTL's are there to maintain safety in the skies, protecting both the pilots and the passengers from the potentially dangerous consequences of tired pilots operating an aircraft.

Airlines must comply with these FTLs, and in many cases, pilot unions negotiate additional restrictions that further limit duty lengths or specify additional protections for pilots.

FTLs limit both the amount of time you can fly for, and the length of time you can be at work, which are known respectively as 'flying hours' and 'duty hours'. The limits were created in collaboration with sleep scientists and fatigue experts, and they were last overhauled across Europe in 2014.

In the UK, some foundational maximum restrictions for flying and duty hours include:

- 900 flying hours each calendar year - This might not sound like much, but as shown in last month's roster example, duty hours far exceed flying hours each day
- 100 flying hours in any 28 consecutive days
- 60 duty hours in any 7 consecutive days
- 95 duty hours in any 14 consecutive days
- 190 duty hours in any 28 consecutive days

While it's good for pilots to have knowledge of these bigger picture limits, the rostering and monitoring software used by airlines should ensure these limits are adhered to.

What pilots contend with more frequently are daily FTLs. These are presented to us in a table format and vary depending on the time your duty started and how many sectors you're operating that day. From the table, Flight Duty Period (FDP) begins at reporting time and ends when the aircraft park brake is set after the final sector.

It's not uncommon to find yourself operating close to these daily limits, particularly during peak periods. But what happens if delays mean you'll exceed these limits before returning to base? This is where 'discretion' comes in.

Discretion

Operating an aircraft beyond the limits laid out in the FTL table is permitted under certain conditions, but it comes with several caveats. Doing so is known as using 'commander's discretion' as it's ultimately a decision that's made by the captain not the company, and it's not one to be taken lightly.

A captain can use discretion to operate a maximum of two hours beyond the limits in the table and must be satisfied that the entire crew are fit and safe to operate beyond these limits. Even then, it's still not expected that this tool will be used.

If a crew chooses not to operate into discretion, it can lead to another crew being called out from standby to operate, or in the worst case, a cancelled flight. You can imagine how this pulls on the heartstrings of the crew. With these decisions, however, emotion must be put to one side and safety put at the forefront. The limits are there for a reason. People make mistakes when they're tired and pilots are no different.

It's also important to note that if an incident occurs during a flight operated under discretion, the captain's decision will likely be highly scrutinised, and it would be their licence and career on the line.

Discretion was designed to be a tool to use in extraordinary circumstances to be able to get your passengers and crew to their destination. In a busy summer working at a short haul operation, you can find yourself having to use discretion multiple times per block in order to complete your duties.

Rest

Airline pilots are also subject to strict regulations regarding rest periods between duties. The term 'minimum rest' refers to the minimum time an airline must give pilots from the end of one duty to the start of the next. In the UK, this is 12 hours.

While this might sound like plenty of time, it's significantly less than the rest periods most 9-to-5 workers get. If you account for an hour commute each way and wish to get an eight hour sleep window, you're left with just an hour each side of your working day for basics like cooking, eating, or family responsibilities.

For pilots operating away from their home base, the minimum rest period can be reduced to just ten hours, further limiting the opportunity for rest. Although still capped at the same flying and duty hour restrictions, long-haul pilots work from slightly different daily FTL tables, based on how acclimatised they are to the time zone they're in.

How Are Airline Rosters Built?

Gone are the days when a human sat down with a spreadsheet to manually assign flying duties. Today, airlines use highly sophisticated software to create rosters for thousands of pilots. The system considers the flying schedule, bidding preferences, and flight time limitations, to produce rosters that comply with these regulations while also optimising crew efficiency.

Airlines still have crewing departments that work extremely hard, but much of their time is spent manipulating this software during delays and disruption to keep the flying operation going.

Vacation Days

Most airlines require pilots to 'bid' for their vacation days, often more than a year in advance. The bidding process varies by airline. Some use a seniority-based system to decide who gets priority, while others consider factors like how successful you were in previous bidding rounds.

After bidding is completed, airlines often allow pilots to book additional leave on a shorter-term basis (still usually a minimum of two to three months in advance). However, these opportunities are usually limited to quieter periods in the flight schedule, meaning weekends and school holidays are often off-limits. The lack of flexibility with vacation scheduling can be a challenge for pilots, particularly those with families or other commitments.

Overtime

Most airlines offer the opportunity to work overtime, giving pilots the chance to operate uncrewed flights on their days off. Pilots on a full-time roster usually work close to their maximum hours anyway, so they'd violate hour restrictions by working on their days off. For those on part-time contracts, however, offering overtime can be a flexible way to earn extra income.

Schedule Summary

To conclude, each roster type comes with a set of advantages and disadvantages. Fixed rosters can offer a semblance of work-life balance. Although pilots on these rosters can't predict their working hours until the middle of the month before, they do know their working days, allowing them to plan their personal lives more effectively.

Flexible rosters can offer pilots fewer working days in a row, and more autonomy in being able to bid for certain days off, however, there's far less predictability, which can make personal life and meeting commitments outside of work challenging.

Whichever roster type a pilot is on, the work can be extremely demanding, often involving long, antisocial hours. The irregular hours, weekend work and last-minute changes can be challenging, especially for those with families.

A unique aspect of this profession, however, is that most pilots get more than just two days off between each working block. As a whole, they usually get more time off than the normal 9-5 worker, giving them more free time and the opportunity to travel or pursue their interests outside of work.

The F Word

I wanted to devote a chapter in this book to the F word, as it's something that's becoming more prevalent in the airline industry, with potentially catastrophic impacts.

If you take one look at a modern day full-time airline pilot's schedule, you'll see that it's almost impossible for a normal human to fulfil that schedule without feeling the effects of exhaustion and extreme tiredness during working hours.

We call this fatigue, and it's potentially lethal. Unfortunately, airlines tend to treat the previously mentioned FTL's as targets to work towards in the name of profit and efficiency, as opposed to limits to stay away from. Consistently working up to and beyond these limits can result in fatigue, which can severely compromise a pilot's performance through impaired decision making and judgement, difficulty concentrating, slowed reaction times and increased irritability. Hopefully you agree that none of these are desirable effects for the person sitting at the pointy end of the jet.

Thankfully, as pilots, we're provided with certain tools to help mitigate the effects of fatigue, however I see them all as a short term fix as opposed to a long term solution. Let's explore these mitigation tools.

Mitigation

The first mitigation tool is a drug. Yep, you've read that right. Just in the form of a legalised one. One 'perk' all airlines (excluding a certain low-cost Irish carrier) give their staff is free tea and coffee while on duty. While this seems like a lovely kind-hearted gesture, what they're really doing is plying their crew with caffeine to help them mitigate their level of tiredness and get them through a working day.

I saw this time and time again as a first officer; knackered captains who would have four or five cups of coffee each day just to help them stay alert. In my first few years as a pilot, I fell into this trap, especially when operating flights deep into the night, far beyond the time my body wanted to still be awake at. I'd get plied with coffee all day, followed by another just before landing to ensure I was alert. After years of struggling to sleep properly, I decided to cut caffeine out completely and my sleep improved no end, as did various other aspects of my life. One negative consequence, however, was that I felt how truly knackered I was during these long duties, something that most pilots cover up with the stimulating drug. It showed me that caffeine is very much a short-term fix to a bigger underlying problem. So, what other tools do we have at our disposal if we don't want to take stimulating drugs to get through a duty?

Sleeping in the flight deck, otherwise known as 'controlled rest', is an extremely helpful tool that we have available to us, but there are various considerations that must be made before using it. It goes without saying that only one pilot can undertake controlled rest at any time. The other must be fully alert as they then become responsible for the aircraft's trajectory, as well as management of the radio communications whist the other pilot dozes. As a safety measure, we are also obliged to inform the cabin crew if one pilot is going to take controlled rest. The procedure they must then follow is to call us every ten minutes instead of every 20 minutes, to ensure the other pilot is still alert and awake.

While I understand the logic behind this, I don't think whoever wrote that rule was aware of how loud the cabin interphone call noise is in the cockpit. If the pilot taking controlled rest does manage to successfully drift into a peaceful sleep in the first ten minutes, they're going to be woken up by the very loud call alert every ten minutes, so they're never really going to get any substantial rest.

Our manuals also state that a period of controlled rest shouldn't allow you to fall into deep sleep and therefore shouldn't last for a period of longer than 20-30 minutes. They also state that due to sleep inertia (still feeling very tired for a period of time after waking up) we must stop any controlled rest long before we commence any descent.

I'll let you decide whether you believe pilots abide fully by the above timing procedures. All I will say is we all take a sensible and logical approach to managing our rest in the flight deck if we need to.

Personally, I'm unable to ever properly fall asleep in the flight deck (possibly quite reassuring to passengers?). I'm unsure whether it's to do with the fact that I can't really switch my brain off when I'm in command of a commercial airliner flying through the air at 500mph, or whether it's due to the fact that our seats don't recline much past 45 degrees so it's not exactly the comfiest position to rest in. Either way, controlled rest is a tool I try to utilise if I feel I need it. It's often the only chance I get all day to close my eyes and not have to focus on anything, which in itself gives the brain a much-needed break. I often feel noticeably more alert after just 15 minutes of closing my eyes and letting my mind wander.

Long haul is slightly different as they usually have multiple crew members rotating between the two flight deck seats and a dedicated rest bunk. They'll have specific pre-agreed rest times for each pilot. I'm reliably informed by many of my long haul friends that on night flights, quite often there will only ever be one pilot awake, even if there are three pilots onboard. If it's just two crew onboard, one of the pilots will be sleeping in the pilot's seat while the other is alert and awake. If it's three crew, there will be another pilot asleep in the crew bunk. These pilots will then rotate every 90 minutes, or at intervals decided by the pilots depending on how they all feel. I'm told that the main challenge of long-haul is more about managing sleep rather than actually operating the aircraft.

Controlled rest, however, shouldn't be something we rely on to get us through a working day, especially in short-haul operations. Imagine doing an office job and saying to your boss that you feel so tired you need to take a 25 minute sleep under your desk to be able to carry on working effectively. Then throw in that in your line of work, if you make a slip up it could potentially cost hundreds or thousands of lives. Seems insane, doesn't it? That's essentially what we're doing.

The final and most underused tool we can use is to refuse to operate due to fatigue. We are well within our rights to do this for any duty, if we genuinely believe that during that duty, we feel the effects of fatigue could endanger the safety of the operation.

It's a great tool, however, it's not used anywhere near as much as it should be for various reasons. Firstly, pride. Pilots are a proud bunch, and I firmly believe airline management play on that. I've seen plenty of very proud pilots state that they've never taken a day off work due to sickness or fatigue. I have an extremely strong work ethic, so I used to aspire to be like these pilots, however I now look at them very differently and think they're actually not so smart. Our rosters are barely fit for human consumption. Add the constant delays, duty changes and various other stressors, and you end up driving yourself into the ground if you don't take control of things and set your own boundaries.

Secondly, fear of negative consequences. Brand new pilots are unlikely to refuse to work due to fatigue, mainly due to the fear (rightly or wrongly) of negative consequences. They've just invested a substantial amount of time and money into training and finally land their first airline job. How likely do you think it is that they'll tell their brand new employer they're too tired to come to work that day?

For those new to the airline world, it's also a culture shift. You can't simply refuse to work most jobs because you're too tired, but then most jobs don't have the same level of responsibility ours does.

With experience and time in the airline world, pilots hopefully learn the importance of managing their own fatigue by refusing duties for this reason. It doesn't have to be a flat out refusal. In my experience, my airline will try to work with me if I'm honest about things. On many occasions I've spoken to our crewing department to let them know I'm feeling absolutely exhausted and don't feel fit to operate an extremely long day that I'm planned for. If they can, they'll look to swap me to a shorter day.

When we go fatigued, we have to submit a safety report to management. The report automatically collates various bits of data, such as the length and start times of our previous duties and produces a 'fatigue score'. This is essentially a score out of five, that should be indicative of how fatigued we may be feeling, based on the last few duty days.

There have been occasions where I've debated hard about whether to go fatigued or not for a certain duty, and after submitting a report, noticed it returned a score of four out of five, i.e. almost the maximum level of fatigue. Why all airlines don't have a system in place that automatically tracks pilots' supposed fatigue levels, and prevents them being allowed to operate with a score that's a four out of five or above is beyond me, although it likely comes down to money.

I can happily say that in ten years of operating for my airline, only once have I been questioned on my decision to refuse a duty based on fatigue. This was due to my fatigue report producing a very low score, however, after a discussion with management, it was deemed I was correct to call fatigued.

Unfortunately, not all airlines are the same. Pilots from other carriers face heavy pressure from their management to avoid refusing duties based on fatigue. There's an infamous leaked video on the internet of Joseph Varadi, the CEO of Wizz Air (a European-based low-cost airline) in an internal staff meeting, telling pilots that the airline can't sustain the current rate at which pilots are calling fatigued. Instead of explaining how the airline plans to build less fatiguing rosters, which would be the expected solution, he goes on to essentially tell pilots to stop refusing duties based on fatigue. Thankfully my airline is nothing like that, however, it's very sad to see that some airlines just don't take this subject seriously and are happy to continue to erode the safety margin in the name of profit.

Solution

So, what's the long term solution here? Airlines viewing maximum flight time limitations as limits to stay well clear of rather than to work towards would be a step in the right direction. Unfortunately, I can't see any airlines taking it upon themselves to do this without a directive from a higher authority.

If one airline decides to do this, they're putting themselves at an immediate competitive disadvantage to other airlines that continue to stretch their crews to and beyond their limits, and therefore can keep their costs lower. In a world where passengers tend to choose their flights based mainly on the price of their tickets, the majority of airlines survive on the ability to keep their costs low.

I believe aviation regulatory bodies should reconsider current regulations and flight time limitations, while ensuring that the airlines prioritise pilot well-being and ultimately safety over profit.

For more detailed information on fatigue and potential solutions, please see my in-depth articles on Pilotbible.com.

FAQ's

Finally, a quickfire round of FAQs will be used to wrap up any common questions that haven't been touched on thus far.

Do all short-haul pilots aspire to be long-haul pilots?

No. Short-haul and long-haul are totally different lifestyles. While pilots usually have to do a few years in short-haul before being able to operate long-haul routes, there are plenty of pilots, myself included, who have no desire to ever fly long-haul.

Each type of operation comes with its own set of challenges and problems to navigate. While the idea of flying a larger jet to glamorous destinations around the globe is quite alluring, the reality of that life isn't one that I'm cut out for. While short-haul operations can be relentless, I enjoy being home in my own bed every night. I also like the flexibility and predictability my part-time roster gives me.

The idea of battling jet lag, sleeping in hotel rooms, and being away from home for days at a time each trip isn't something I want in my life. I also know that I'd get extremely bored with the actual operation itself – essentially flying on autopilot up to 12 hours at a time and only getting to do a few landings per month.

I have friends in the long-haul world who are extremely happy, and you couldn't pay them enough to come over to the short-haul world. Everyone's different and enjoys different things. As a pilot, it's important you understand what both lifestyles really consist of and what you want out of the job in order to ensure you end up in the right sort of operation.

I've also had many friends that have jumped between short-haul and long-haul, and then back again, so you can always change if you end up not enjoying what you do.

Do airline pilots always fly to the same place?

No. For short-haul pilots, each day will usually be a different destination to the previous. For long haul, each trip will likely be different. The only real caveat is if you're in a very small airline with few destinations or are extremely senior and bid for the same destination each month.

Do airline pilots choose which flights they operate?

While pilots can 'bid' for specific flights, the likelihood of getting it depends on their seniority at a seniority-based airline. For first officers or new pilots, this will be hard. Senior pilots in a seniority-based airline will often get what they bid for, so they can usually design most of their own roster.

Do you get better schedules the longer you stay at an airline?

In a seniority-based airline you do.

Can airlines change your roster after it's published?

Yes. At short-haul airlines during peak periods, quite often the roster you're first given looks drastically different to the one you end up flying. The company can change your duty right up to the time you report. This can understandably lead to challenges when it comes to scheduling life around work.

Can pilots swap duties with each other?

Yes. Most airlines have systems in place for this, however, due to the number of regulations and limitations, there's usually a very slim chance the swap will be approved by the system due to it not fitting in with the rest of their block of work.

How do pilot salaries work?

This is a big question that I'll dedicate an entire blog post to on Pilotbible.com. It's also detailed in my other book 'How to Become an Airline Pilot' along with real examples of payslips for both captains and first officers, but to summarise:

Pay varies hugely, airline to airline, and country to country. It varies further based on flight experience, time with the company, the type of aircraft you fly, and which seat you're sitting in.

Often, pilots will receive a 'basic' salary, which they get paid whether they fly or not. On top of that, they'll receive some form of additional compensation each time they fly. This could be 'sector pay'- paid per sector flown, usually varying in amount depending on the physical distance of the sector. Alternatively, it could be more time-based, with pay linked to each minute spent at work.

Pilots will usually get additional payment for any standby or simulator duties completed. Pilots may also be eligible for performance bonuses each year if the company achieves good profits. Some airlines offer loyalty bonuses to their staff, which increase annually based on how long they've been with the company.

What's the future of the airline pilot role?

Much to the dismay of many current airline pilots, major manufacturers are currently working on building aircraft that would allow for single pilot operations. While pilot unions are fighting this hard, I believe it will be the future, and unions should embrace this and work with the manufacturers to make the shift as sustainable and safe as possible rather than fighting it outright.

I believe that, in the short term, we'll see large airliners operated by single pilots rather than an entire flight crew within the next 10 years. Over the long term, I believe AI will find its place in the flight deck, and eventually, the need for a pilot will be removed completely. How far off that is, is anyone's guess. Although many people state 'I'd never get on an aircraft that didn't have a human pilot onboard', when you consider that the majority of aviation accidents are caused by human error and that there will be a day where computers can operate aircraft with a smaller margin of error than humans, it makes total sense that this is the future of flying. I think there will be a ground-based pilot who's responsible for monitoring many aircraft at once and is able to intervene remotely if needed. That's just my opinion. Let's see what happens...

Thank you for reading! If you enjoyed the book, I'd really appreciate it if you could take two minutes to leave a very quick review on Amazon. It helps more than you know!

Scan To Review

About The Author

I'm Sam, an airline captain with one of Europe's largest airlines, operating Airbus A320s around their network for over ten years. I've been fascinated with aviation since before I could talk and have been flying airliners since I left school. I've quickly progressed through the ranks by putting in lots of hard work and dedication to become one of the youngest captains and instructors within the airline.

A few years ago, I decided to focus heavily on my writing, to share my experiences and create resources to help others that may wish to follow my path. I created PilotBible.com – an online community where pilots can share their own stories and insights into different roles to help future and current pilots.

I'd like to personally thank you for purchasing this book. It's taken a long time to develop it from a messy first draft to a hopefully much more refined finished copy that's enjoyable and insightful to read. The success of my first book *How to Become an Airline Pilot* blew me away, and every time someone purchases this latest book, it encourages me to continue creating and sharing my work.

Please check out our discount & recommendations section on PilotBible.com for the latest deals we've negotiated with the big names out there.

If you have any questions or feedback, please feel free to email or get in touch via our social channels, and I'll endeavour to get back to you.

Check Out Our Amazon Bestsellers

How To Become An Airline Pilot: The Definitive Step by Step Guide

Scan To View

If you're interested in pursuing a career path as an airline pilot, I've put together an entire guide that is kept up-to-date each year, explaining how you can make your dream a reality. This in-depth guide walks you through all the specifics of entering the airline world. It helps you pass the selection process and gives you the best chance of landing the airline job you want.

How To Become A Pilot: The Ultimate Step by Step Guide

If you know you want to fly but are unsure which flying role is right for you, this book breaks down every flying role out there. The pros, cons and everything in between. It's a great way to explore all the options out there and how to best set yourself up for success in them.

Scan To View

Both books are available in e-book and paperback on Amazon and with all major aviation retailers. To get notified when we release more books, subscribe for free at PilotBible.com.

Printed in Dunstable, United Kingdom